101
BEAR 4-6 STUNTS

Leo Hand and Phil Johnson

ISBN: 1-58518-841-7
Library of Congress Control Number: 2003100643
Cover design: Kerry Hartjen
Book layout: Deborah Oldenburg
Diagrams: Donnie Laffoday
Front cover photo: Jonathan Daniel/Getty Images

Coaches Choice
PO Box 1828
Monterey, CA 93942
www.coacheschoice.com

DEDICATION

For
Bob, Dessa, AJ, Alysha, Joe Griffin
and the '89 State Champion Serra Cavaliers

–Leo Hand

For
Caren

–Phil Johnson

ACKNOWLEDGMENTS

Thanks to my wife, Mary, who urged me to follow my heart
even though it involved sacrifice and risk for her.

Thanks to the offspring whose ancestors endured the *Middle Chamber*
and the *Long Walk* for all of the contributions that they have made
to the greatest game of all.

–Leo Hand

Thanks to my co-author, Leo Hand.

–Phil Johnson

CONTENTS

INTRODUCTION

What's in This Book for You

This book provides the reader with the following information:

- Eleven innovative stunt tactics that will enable a defense to actually attack the offense.
- An explanation of the assignments and techniques necessary to install football's newest defensive innovation–the fire zone blitz.
- 101 explosive stunts from a variety of man and zone pass coverages.
- A variety of examples showing how to adapt the eleven stunt strategies to aceback and empty formations.
- A thorough explanation of the assignments and techniques necessary to implement both man and zone pass coverages.
- A synopsis of the Bear 46 base responsibilities.

Before We Begin

There are a few terms that will constantly be referred to throughout the text. Because different phrases and words can sometimes mean different things to different people, the following terms are defined and clarified as they are used in this book:

- **Strongside/weakside:** The strongside is toward the tight end, and the weakside is toward the split end. Strong defenders (example: strong tackle) are aligned on the tight-end side, and weak defenders are aligned on the split-end side.
- Player position names are as illustrated in Figure Intro-1.

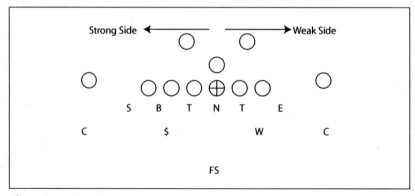

Figure Intro-1

- □ **Strong cornerback**–the cornerback who lines up opposite the flanker.
- □ **Weak cornerback**–the cornerback who lines up opposite the split end.
- □ **Strong safety ($)**–*the adjuster.* The defensive back/linebacker who lines up as an inside linebacker.
- □ **Free safety (FS)**–the safety who is aligned in center field.
- □ **Stud**–the outside linebacker who lines up toward the strongside in an 8 technique.
- □ **Buck**–the outside linebacker who lines up toward the strongside in a 7 technique.
- □ **Strong tackle**–the defensive tackle who lines up on the strongside in a 3 technique.
- □ **Nose**–the defensive lineman who lines up opposite the center in a 0 technique.
- □ **Weak tackle**–the defensive tackle who lines up on the weakside in a 3 technique.
- □ **Whip**–the inside linebacker who lines up on the weakside.

- **Gap Responsibilities** are lettered as illustrated in Figure Intro-2.

Figure Intro-2

- **Alignments** are numbered as illustrated in Figure Intro-3.

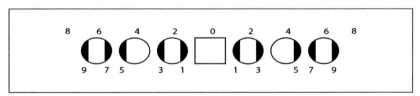

Figure Intro-3

- **Receivers** are numbered as illustrated in Figure Intro-4.

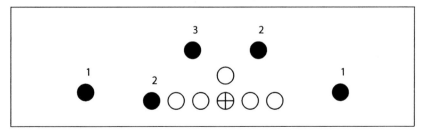

Figure Intro-4

CHAPTER 1

Eleven Stunt Strategies that Win Games

Illusion Blitzes

The term blitz refers to a stunt that employs a 6-man pass rush. An illusion blitz is a specific type of blitz that gives the offense the *illusion* that the defense is "sending the house." When an illusion blitz is employed, seven or eight defenders attack the line of scrimmage at the snap. Against the run, these seven or eight defenders attempt to penetrate the gaps, control the line of scrimmage, force the ball carrier out of his intended course, and ultimately stop the play in the backfield. Against the pass, six of the defenders continue to rush the quarterback and the remaining one or two *fake* pass rushers *spy* the running back(s). Against the pass, illusion blitzes hold the offense accountable for blocking all seven or eight defenders aligned in the box, thereby limiting the number of receivers an offense can put into pass patterns and still safely protect the quarterback. Furthermore, illusion blitzes make pass protection a chaotic guessing game. Since the *spy* defenders are often defensive linemen, illusion blitzes not only cause offensive linemen to end up *blocking air*, they also eliminate many protection schemes that require offensive linemen to *double read* defensive alignments. Illusion Blitzes are employed with zero coverage. Figure 1-1 illustrates an illusion blitz in which eight defenders are attacking the line of scrimmage at the snap, but as they recognize pass, two of the defenders *spy* the two running backs. If the running backs block instead of releasing for a pattern, the two *spy* defenders continue as *fake rushers*. It is vital that the *fake rushers* understand that spying the running backs takes precedence over *pretending* to rush the quarterback, otherwise, they may become vulnerable to delay pass routes or screen patterns.

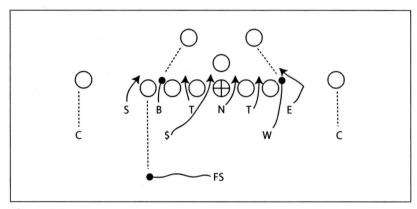

Figure 1-1

Blitzes

Illusion blitzes are usually called when the offense is expected to pass. Blitzes, on the other hand, are usually called in run situations. Many coaches use blitzes to pressure the offense from the edge and free up the two inside linebackers so that they can pursue the ball carrier from an inside-out position. Like illusion blitzes, blitzes are used with zero coverage. Figure 1-2 illustrates a popular Bear 46 blitz.

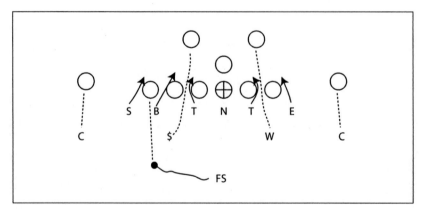

Figure 1-2

Illusion Dogs

The term *dog* refers to a stunt that employs a 5-man pass rush. Figure 1-3 shows a common Bear 46 illusion dog. Illusion dogs are almost identical to illusion blitzes. The two differences between these two tactics are:

- Illusion dogs employ 5-man pass rushes and illusion blitzes employ 6-man pass rushes.

- Cover 1 is used with illusion dogs and zero coverage is used with illusion blitzes. Although illusion dogs put less pressure on a quarterback, many coaches feel more secure using them because their defense is afforded the luxury of a free safety who backs up the defenders in the box and plays center field versus the pass.

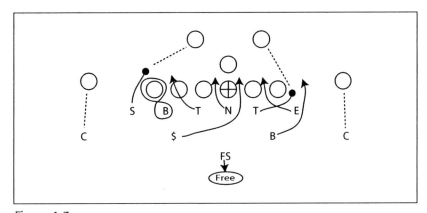

Figure 1-3

Dogs

Dogs and blitzes are like illusion dogs and illusion blitzes in their similarities and differences. Figure 1-4 shows a common Bear 46 dog.

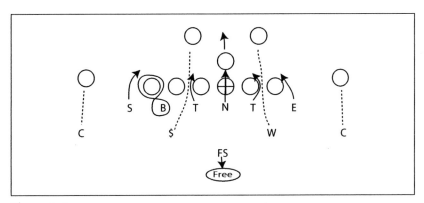

Figure 1-4

Fire Zone Blitzes

Fire zone blitzes are not really blitzes; they're actually dogs because they involve five-man pass rushes, and they're used with cover 1. However, since fire zone blitz has become the universal term used to describe this tactic, it will be used in this book. A fire zone blitz is a variation of an illusion dog. Unlike illusion dogs however, fire zone blitzes have three defenders drop off into the under coverage and combo cover the tight end and two running backs versus pass. The areas that these three defenders drop off into will be referred to in this book as **Abel**, **Baker**, and **Charlie**. In addition to all of the advantages gained by using illusion blitzes and dogs, fire zone blitzes often cause the quarterback to quickly dump the ball off to a *hot* receiver in a long passing situation. This frequently results in the offense failing to gain a first down. The specifics of the fire zone blitz are discussed in a later chapter. Figure 1-5 shows a common Bear 46 fire zone blitz.

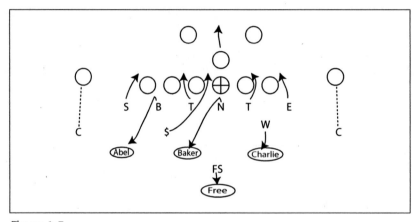

Figure 1-5

Hybrid Fire Zone Blitzes

This tactic combines a strongside fire zone concept with a weakside illusion. Figure 1-6 illustrates a Bear 46 hybrid fire zone blitz in which the nose and Stud drop off into coverage and combo-cover the tight end and strong halfback (similar to a fire zone **Abel-Baker** drop) while the weak end *spies* the weakside halfback.

Old School Zone Blitzes

Back when Tom Bass was coaching in the NFL, he frequently blitzed linebackers and dropped defensive linemen into coverage. Unlike today's fire zone blitz, the pass coverage Coach Bass used to implement this tactic was a two- or three-deep zone. Figure 1-7 shows an *old school* zone blitz using a variation of cover 3 in which the nose and weak end drop off into coverage.

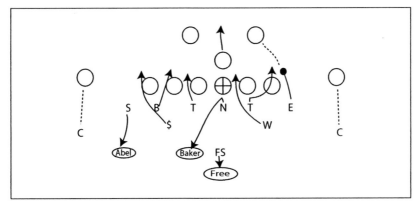

Figure 1-6

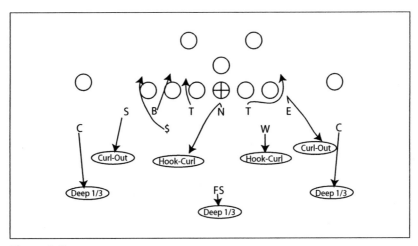

Figure 1-7

Overloads

Overloads attempt to get more pass rushers on one side of the ball than available pass blockers. Both strongside and weakside overloads are easily attainable using the Bear 46 by having a defensive lineman or linebacker employ a delayed pass rush. Figure 1-8 shows a strongside overload that is created by a delayed pass rush by the nose. This delayed rush by the nose puts the defense in the dilemma of trying to block four pass rushers (*illusion* of five rushers) with three pass blockers. The only way that the offense can resolve this problem is to use both the tight end and strongside halfback as pass blockers, or have the quarterback quickly dump the ball off to one of the receivers.

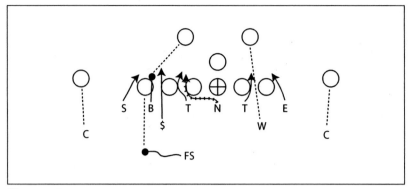

Figure 1-8

Line Twists

Line twists have always been an effective weapon versus both pass and run. Line twists can occur as the ball is being snapped, or they can be implemented as delayed reactions to pass. Figure 1-9 illustrates a line twist that occurs as the ball is snapped. This line twist is shown being used in conjunction with a dog.

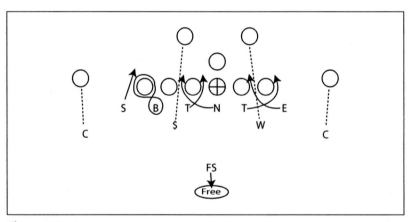

Figure 1-9

Secondary Blitzes

Secondary blitzes and fake secondary blitzes are powerful multifaceted weapons that can easily be incorporated into a multitude of Bear 46 blitz and illusion blitz schemes. Figure 1-10 shows a free safety blitz that is incorporated into a blitz scheme.

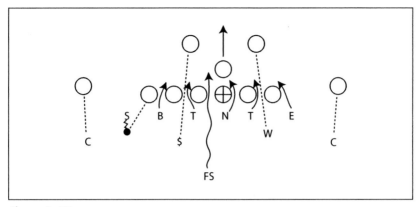

Figure 1-10

Twin Stunts

Whenever two players stunt through the same gap, it is referred to as a twin stunt. Defensive backs, linebackers, or linemen can be used to create twin stunts. Figure 1-11 shows a *twin stunt* that is achieved by the strong safety delay blitzing through the weakside A gap with the nose (the overload shown in Figure 1-8 is accomplished by a twin stunt involving the strong tackle and nose). This is an unusual tactic. Since few offensive teams ever see this type of stunt, it is often very effective. Twin stunts are usually called in passing situations.

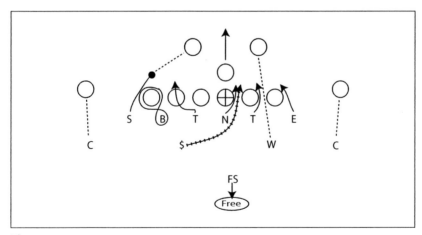

Figure 1-11

CHAPTER 2

Basic Principles of Blitzing

- If a player blitzes infrequently, using it as an element of surprise, it's important that he disguises his intention.

- If a player frequently blitz, disguising his intention may not be as important because he may want to occasionally give the offense a false key by *showing blitz* but then *playing straight* at the snap of the ball. Whichever strategy he decides to use, it is important that he does not establish a pattern that can be exploited.

- A player's eyes are one of his most important tools when blitzing. To be an effective blitzer, a player must be able to see (on the run) the keys that that will lead him to the ball. Seeing these keys is the first step in being able to read and react to them.

- Unless the blitz is a delayed reaction to a pass, it is critical that the blitzer is moving, attacking, and penetrating the line of scrimmage at the snap of the ball.

- A blitzer must keep his feet moving at all times. This is especially important when he becomes engaged with a blocker.

- A blitzing player should use his quickness in an attempt to avoid blockers.

- If the play is a pass, and the blitzer becomes engaged with a blocker, he should keep his hands inside of the blocker's hands and try to maintain separation from the blocker. He should not look at the passer too soon, or he may lose sight of the blocker. The blitzer must first defeat the blocker before he can sack the quarterback. While a blitzer should have a predetermined pass rush move in mind, he should be ready to change his move according to the circumstances. A blitzer needs to take what the blocker gives him and make his move at the appropriate time. Remember that if a blitzing player makes his pass rush move too soon, the blocker will have time to recover. On the other hand, if he makes his move too late, he will probably be too close to the blocker, thereby enabling the blocker to get into the blitzer's body and nullify his charge. If possible, the blitzer should try to get the blocker turned one way and then make his move in the opposite direction. The blitzing player should also use his forward momentum to manipulate the blocker's momentum. If the blocker's momentum is back, the blitzer should attack him with a power move and knock him backwards. If his momentum is forward, the player can use a move that puts the blocker forward and destroys his balance. A blitzing player should never leave his feet to bat a ball down. He should get his hands up as the quarterback begins his throwing motion, but continue his charge toward the quarterback. Too often, when a defender jumps up to bat a pass down, the quarterback will duck under, elude the defender, and scramble out of the pocket.

- If the play is a run, a blitzer should react to his keys and the pressure of blocks as he normally would if he were employing a read technique. Since a blitzer has forward momentum to his advantage, he should use his hands rather than his forearm when attacking a blocker. A blitzing player should maintain separation from blockers and not let them get into his legs. If possible, blitzers should try to make the blocker miss.

- When blitzing, a player should keep his body under control at all times, try to maintain a low center of gravity and provide as small a target as possible for the blockers.

- Blitzers need to study their opponents' game films carefully. They should know how their potential blockers react and what techniques they favor. It helps to know the strengths and weaknesses of the opponent.

- A blitzer should also study his opponent's eyes as he's getting set at the line of scrimmage. The blocker's eyes will often tell a blitzer where he's going. Studying the pressure that the blocker puts on his down hand when he gets into his stances will also frequently give a pass/run or a directional key.

- Blitzers who study the scouting report will increase their knowledge of the opponents' formation, down-and-distance, and field-position tendencies. They should use this information to anticipate, but never to guess.

- All players should gang tackle and try to strip the ball out of the ball carrier's arm. Players should never take for granted that a running back or quarterback has been downed. If they arrive at a pile late, they should be on the alert for a loose ball.

- Players must maintain total intensity from the time the ball is snapped until the whistle is blown.

- Before the snap, a blitzer should anticipate potential blockers and be prepared to react to those blockers as he penetrates the line.

- On plays directed toward a blitzer's side of the field, he should make the tackle. On plays directed away from him, he should take the proper angle of pursuit and be in on the tackle. Players should always pursue relentlessly. Remember that if a player is not within five yards of the ball when the whistle blows he is probably loafing.

- If the backfield action does not indicate flow, a blitzer should protect his gap until he finds the ball. He should never guess.

- If a player is assigned to *spy* (cover a back) when he's blitzing, he should expect that the back will first block and then run a delayed route. Do not allow him to be fooled. Remind him that he must cover the back, no matter what the back does, until the whistle blows.

- The ball is the blitzer's trigger. When the ball is snapped, *he's gone!* He should not listen to an opponent's cadence; they're not talking to him!

- Players should not rely upon the lines that are marked on the field. The ball, not the lines, establishes the line of scrimmage.

CHAPTER 3

Zero Coverage Stunts

When zero coverage is employed, there will be no free safeties. The three defensive backs will be assigned to guard the tight end and two wide receivers man-to-man, and two defenders in the box will be assigned to cover the two running backs. Zero coverage is used with blitzes and illusion blitzes.

The strength of the zero coverage strategy is that it has six defenders (blitz scheme) or seven/eight defenders (illusion blitz scheme) attacking gaps and penetrating the line of scrimmage. Its weakness is that all of the secondary defenders are locked on receivers and none are keying the ball; therefore, if a runner breaks the line of scrimmage or a defensive back gets beat deep, there is a good chance that a touchdown will result. Despite this weakness, zero coverage can cause an offense a lot of problems, especially when the defenders in the box have some "quicks," and the defensive backs are skillful man-to-man pass defenders.

Secondary Man-Man Techniques for Zero Coverage

Stance and Alignment

A defensive secondary player should:

- Align himself with an inside shade on the receiver, approximately seven yards deep.

- Set up with a narrow base, feet inside of his armpits, outside foot up (toe-heel relationship).
- Keep his weight on his front foot.
- Keep his knees bent and his hips lowered.
- Slightly round his back with his head and shoulders over his front foot (nose over the toes).
- Allow his arms to hang loose.
- See both the receiver and quarterback with his peripheral vision.

Backpedal

A defensive secondary player should:

- Maintain inside leverage on the receiver.
- Keep a good forward lean as he backpedals (chin down and nose over the toes).
- Push off with his front foot and take his first step with his back foot. He should never step forward or lift a foot and set it back down in the same place.
- Keep his weight on the balls of his feet.
- Reach back with each step and pull his weight over his feet.
- Keep his feet close to the ground during the backpedal.
- Not over-stride; take small-to-medium steps.
- Keep his arms bent at a 90-degree angle—relaxed, but pumping vigorously.
- Maintain a proper cushion. When the receiver gets 10 yards downfield, the defender should be 15 yards deep. When the receiver is 15 yards downfield, the defender should be 18 yards deep.
- Remember and anticipate that 3-step routes are usually thrown five to seven yards downfield (the exception being the fade); 5-step patterns are thrown 8-15 yards downfield; and 7-step routes are usually thrown 18+ yards downfield.
- Be aware of a receiver's split. Wide splits often indicate inside routes; tight splits often indicate outside routes.
- Keep his shoulders parallel to the line and not let the receiver turn him.
- Mirror the receiver's movements while keeping his own outside shoulder on the receiver's inside shoulder. He must not let the receiver get head up with him.
- Control the speed of his backpedal. When the receiver makes his break, the defender must be under control and able to gather and break quickly in the direction of the break.
- Concentrate on the base of the receiver's numbers until he makes his final break.

- Anticipate a break when the receiver changes his forward lean, begins to chop his feet, or begins to widen his base.

- Honor all inside fakes.

- Not backpedal at the snap if aligned on a tight end. Be ready to jump a flat or crossing route. If the tight end goes vertical, the defender must work to an inside-leverage position.

- Remember that "if the receiver gets even (with the defender), he's leavin'." Whenever a receiver gets too close, the defender must turn and run with him, keeping his body between the receiver and the ball. He must not allow separation to occur. As he's running with the receiver, he can try to disrupt the receiver's strides by slapping at his near hand and wrist.

Plant and Drive

- When the receiver makes his final break, the defensive back should drop his shoulder in the direction of the receiver's break and explode in that direction. He must make his break parallel to the receiver's break, and quickly close the cushion.

- The defender must not loose concentration on the receiver. He should not look for the ball until he's closed his cushion and he sees the receiver look for the ball.

- If the receiver tries to change direction after the defender has begun his drive, the defensive player should be in a position so that the receiver will have to make contact with him in order to change directions.

Playing the Ball

A defensive secondary player should:

- Attack the ball at its highest point.

- Play the ball, not the receiver, when the ball is to his inside and the receiver is outside of him.

- Play the ball through the receiver's upfield shoulder when the receiver is between him and the ball. He should never cut in front of the receiver to make an interception unless he is sure that he can get two hands on the ball.

- Try to catch the ball or break up a pass with two hands, not one.

- Always knock the ball toward the ground, never up in the air.

- Try to strip the ball if the receiver catches the pass.

- Head to the nearest sideline after intercepting a pass.

- Always look the ball into his hands and protect it after he catches it.

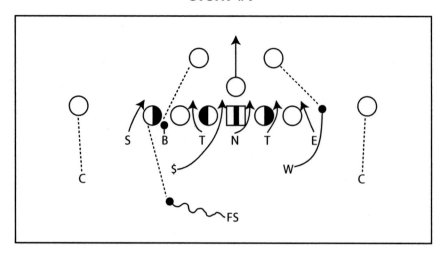

STUNT DESCRIPTION: This is an *illusion blitz.*

SECONDARY COVERAGE: Zero coverage disguised as cover 1. Buck and Whip spy the running backs.

STUD: Rushes from the edge. Contains the quarterback and strongside run. Chases weakside run.

BUCK: Plays 7 technique versus run. Spies the near back versus pass.

STRONG SAFETY: Blitzes through the strongside A gap.

STRONG TACKLE: Slants to the B gap.

NOSE: Slants to the weakside A gap.

WEAK TACKLE: Slants to the B gap.

WEAK END: Attacks the near shoulder of the offensive tackle. Secures the C gap versus run and contains the quarterback versus pass.

WHIP: Fake blitzes to the D gap. Contains the quarterback and weakside run. Chases strongside run.

FREE SAFETY: Covers the tight end. Disguises his assignment as cover 1.

STRONG CORNER: Covers the flanker (inside technique).

WEAK CORNER: Covers the split end (inside technique).

STUNT #2

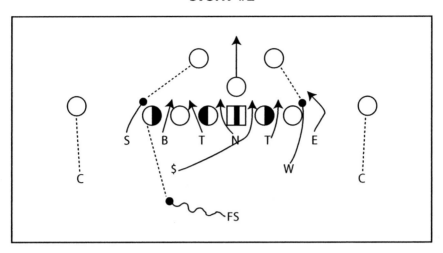

STUNT DESCRIPTION: This is an *illusion blitz*.

SECONDARY COVERAGE: Zero coverage disguised as cover. Stud and Whip spy the running backs.

STUD: Gives the impression that he's rushing from the edge. Contains strongside run and chases weakside run. Spies the near back versus pass.

BUCK: Attacks the near shoulder of the offensive tackle. Secures the C gap versus run and contains the quarterback versus pass.

STRONG SAFETY: Blitzes through the weakside A gap.

STRONG TACKLE: Slants to the B gap.

NOSE: Slants to the strongside A gap.

WEAK TACKLE: Slants to the B gap.

WEAK END: Slants to the D gap. Contains the quarterback and weakside run. Chases strongside run.

WHIP: Attacks the outside shoulder of the offensive tackle. Controls the C gap and spies the near back.

FREE SAFETY: Covers the tight end. Disguises his assignment as cover 1.

STRONG CORNER: Covers the flanker (inside technique).

WEAK CORNER: Covers the split end (inside technique).

STUNT #3

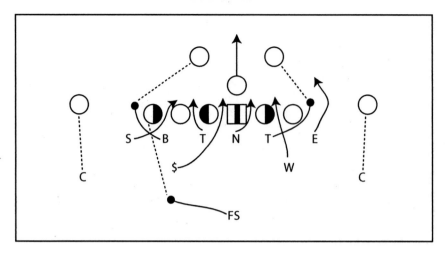

STUNT DESCRIPTION: This is an *illusion blitz*.

SECONDARY COVERAGE: Zero coverage disguised as cover 1. Buck and the weak tackle spy the running backs.

STUD: Loops behind Buck into the strongside C gap. Secures this gap versus run and contains the quarterback versus pass.

BUCK: Slants across the face of the tight end into the D gap. Contains strongside run and chases weakside run. Spies the near back versus pass.

STRONG SAFETY: Blitzes through the strongside A gap.

STRONG TACKLE: Slants to the B gap.

NOSE: Slants to the weakside A gap.

WEAK TACKLE: Slants across the face of the offensive tackle and secures the weakside C gap versus run. Spies the near back versus pass.

WEAK END: Slants to the D gap. Contains weakside run and chases strongside run. Contains the quarterback versus pass.

WHIP: Blitzes through the weakside B gap.

FREE SAFETY: Covers the tight end. Disguises his assignment as cover 1.

STRONG CORNER: Covers the flanker (inside technique).

WEAK CORNER: Covers the split end (inside technique).

STUNT #4

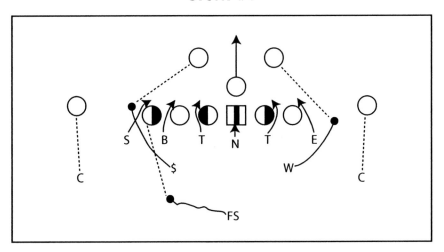

STUNT DESCRIPTION: This is an *illusion blitz*.

SECONDARY COVERAGE: Zero coverage disguised as cover 1. Whip and the strong safety spy the running backs.

STUD: Attacks the tight end's outside shoulder and secures this area versus strongside run. Chases weakside run and contains the quarterback versus pass.

BUCK: Slants through the outside shoulder of the offensive tackle and secures the C gap.

STRONG SAFETY: Scrapes outside. Contains strongside run and chases weakside run. Spies the near back versus pass.

STRONG TACKLE: Plays 3 technique

NOSE: Plays 0 technique

WEAK TACKLE: Plays 3 technique

WEAK END: Attacks the outside shoulder of the offensive tackle. Secures the C gap versus run and contains the quarterback versus pass.

WHIP: Scrapes outside. Contains weakside run and chases strongside run. Spies the near back versus pass.

FREE SAFETY: Covers the tight end. Disguises his assignment as cover 1.

STRONG CORNER: Covers the flanker (inside technique).

WEAK CORNER: Covers the split end (inside technique).

STUNT #5

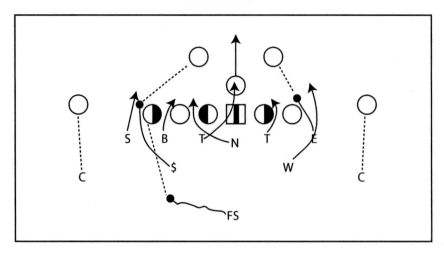

STUNT DESCRIPTION: This *illusion blitz* is augmented by a strongside line twist.

SECONDARY COVERAGE: Zero coverage disguised as cover 1. The strong safety and weak end spy the running backs.

STUD: Rushes from the edge. Contains the quarterback and strongside run. Chases weakside run.

BUCK: Slants through the outside shoulder of the offensive tackle and secures the C gap.

STRONG SAFETY: Attacks the tight end's outside shoulder and secures this area versus run. Spies the near back versus pass.

STRONG TACKLE: Slants to the near shoulder of the center and secures both A gaps.

NOSE: Loops behind the tackle into the strongside B gap.

WEAK TACKLE: Plays 3 technique

WEAK END: Attacks the outside shoulder of the offensive tackle. Secures the C gap versus run and spies the near back versus pass.

WHIP: Scrapes outside. Contains the quarterback and weakside run. Chases strongside run.

FREE SAFETY: Covers the tight end. Disguises his assignment as cover 1.

STRONG CORNER: Covers the flanker (inside technique).

WEAK CORNER: Covers the split end (inside technique).

STUNT #6

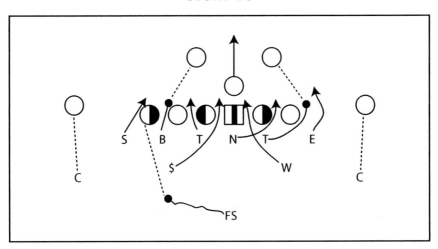

STUNT DESCRIPTION: This is an *illusion blitz*.

SECONDARY COVERAGE: Zero coverage disguised as cover 1. Buck and the weak tackle spy the running backs.

STUD: Rushes from the edge. Contains the quarterback and strongside run. Chases weakside run.

BUCK: Slants through the outside shoulder of the offensive tackle, secures the C gap versus run, and spies the near back versus pass.

STRONG SAFETY: Blitzes through the strongside A gap.

STRONG TACKLE: Slants to the B gap.

NOSE: Slants to the far shoulder of the offensive guard and controls the weakside B gap.

WEAK TACKLE: Slants to the far shoulder of the offensive tackle, secures the C gap versus run, and spies the near back versus pass.

WEAK END: Slants to the D gap. Contains the quarterback and weakside run. Chases strongside run.

WHIP: Blitzes through the weakside A gap.

FREE SAFETY: Covers the tight end. Disguises his assignment as cover 1.

STRONG CORNER: Covers the flanker (inside technique).

WEAK CORNER: Covers the split end (inside technique).

STUNT #7

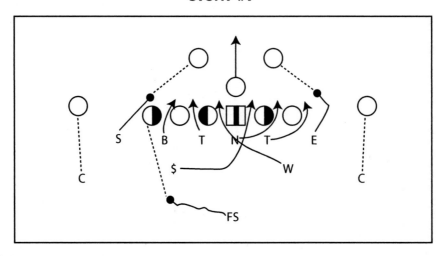

STUNT DESCRIPTION: This is an *illusion blitz*.

SECONDARY COVERAGE: Zero coverage disguised as cover 1. Stud and the weak end spy the running backs.

STUD: Rushes from the edge. Contains strongside run and chases weakside run. Spies the near back versus pass.

BUCK: Slants through the outside shoulder of the offensive tackle, secures the C gap versus run, and contains the quarterback versus pass.

STRONG SAFETY: Blitzes through the weakside A gap (Whip goes first).

STRONG TACKLE: Slants to the B gap.

NOSE: Slants to the far shoulder of the offensive guard and controls the weakside B gap.

WEAK TACKLE: Slants to the far shoulder of the offensive tackle, secures the C gap versus run, and contains the quarterback versus pass.

WEAK END: Slants outside and contains weakside run. Chases strongside run and spies the near back versus pass.

WHIP: Blitzes through the strongside A gap.

FREE SAFETY: Covers the tight end. Disguises his assignment as cover 1.

STRONG CORNER: Covers the flanker (inside technique).

WEAK CORNER: Covers the split end (inside technique).

STUNT #8

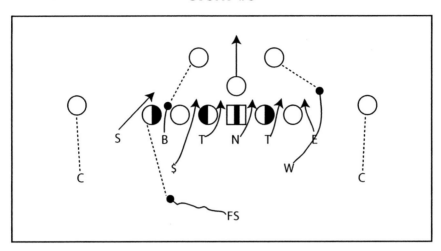

STUNT DESCRIPTION: This is an *illusion blitz*.

SECONDARY COVERAGE: Zero coverage disguised as cover 1. Buck and Whip spy the running backs.

STUD: Rushes from the edge. Contains the quarterback and strongside run. Chases weakside run.

BUCK: Slants through the outside shoulder of the offensive tackle. Secures the C gap versus run and spies the near back versus pass.

STRONG SAFETY: Blitzes through the outside shoulder of the offensive guard and secures the B gap.

STRONG TACKLE: Slants to the A gap.

NOSE: Slants to the weakside A gap.

WEAK TACKLE: Slants to the B gap.

WEAK END: Attacks the near shoulder of the offensive tackle. Secures the C gap versus run and contains the quarterback versus pass.

WHIP: Scrapes outside. Contains weakside run and chases strongside run. Spies the near back versus pass.

FREE SAFETY: Covers the tight end. Disguises his assignment as cover 1.

STRONG CORNER: Covers the flanker (inside technique).

WEAK CORNER: Covers the split end (inside technique).

STUNT # 9

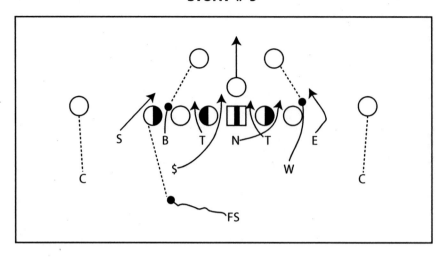

STUNT DESCRIPTION: This *illusion blitz* is enhanced by a weakside line twist.

SECONDARY COVERAGE: Zero coverage disguised as cover 1. Buck and Whip spy the running backs.

STUD: Rushes from the edge. Contains the quarterback and strongside run. Chases weakside run.

BUCK: Slants through the outside shoulder of the offensive tackle. Secures the C gap versus run and spies the near back versus pass.

STRONG SAFETY: Blitzes through the strongside A gap.

STRONG TACKLE: Slants to the B gap.

NOSE: Loops behind the tackle and attacks the far shoulder of the offensive guard. Controls the weakside B gap.

WEAK TACKLE: Slants to the A gap.

WEAK END: Slants outside and contains the quarterback and weakside run. Chases strongside run.

WHIP: Attacks the outside shoulder of the offensive tackle and secures the C gap versus run. Spies the near back versus pass.

FREE SAFETY: Covers the tight end. Disguises his assignment as cover 1.

STRONG CORNER: Covers the flanker (inside technique).

WEAK CORNER: Covers the split end (inside technique).

STUNT #10

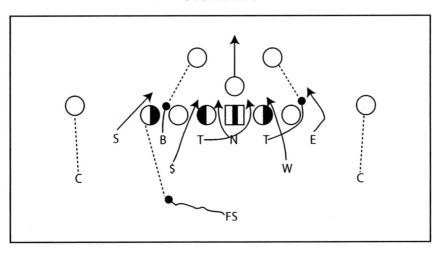

STUNT DESCRIPTION: This *illusion blitz* is enhanced by a weakside line twist.

SECONDARY COVERAGE: Zero coverage disguised as cover 1. Buck and the weak tackle spy the running backs.

STUD: Rushes from the edge. Contains the quarterback and strongside run. Chases weakside run.

BUCK: Slants through the outside shoulder of the offensive tackle. Secures the C gap versus run and spies the near back versus pass.

STRONG SAFETY: Blitzes through the strongside B gap.

STRONG TACKLE: Loops behind the nose into the weakside A gap.

NOSE: Slants into the strongside A gap.

WEAK TACKLE: Slants to the far shoulder of the offensive tackle and controls the weakside C gap versus run. Spies the near back versus pass.

WEAK END: Slants outside and contains the quarterback and weakside run. Chases strongside run.

WHIP: Blitzes through the weakside B gap.

FREE SAFETY: Covers the tight end. Disguises his assignment as cover 1.

STRONG CORNER: Covers the flanker (inside technique).

WEAK CORNER: Covers the split end (inside technique).

STUNT #11

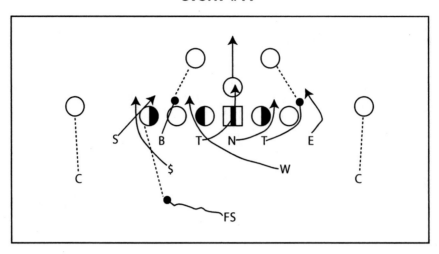

STUNT DESCRIPTION: This is an *illusion blitz*.

SECONDARY COVERAGE: Zero coverage disguised as cover 1. Buck and the weak tackle spy the running backs.

STUD: Attacks the tight end's outside shoulder and secures this area against run. Contains the quarterback versus pass.

BUCK: Slants through the outside shoulder of the offensive tackle and secures the C gap versus run. Spies the near back versus pass.

STRONG SAFETY: Scrapes outside. Contains the quarterback and strongside run. Chases weakside run.

STRONG TACKLE: Attacks the center and controls both A gaps.

NOSE: Slants to the far shoulder of the offensive guard and secures the weakside B gap.

WEAK TACKLE: Slants to the far shoulder of the offensive tackle, secures the C gap versus run, and spies the near back versus pass.

WEAK END: Slants outside and contains the quarterback and weakside run. Chases strongside run.

WHIP: Blitzes through the strongside B gap.

FREE SAFETY: Covers the tight end. Disguises his assignment as cover 1.

STRONG CORNER: Covers the flanker (inside technique).

WEAK CORNER: Covers the split end (inside technique).

STUNT #12

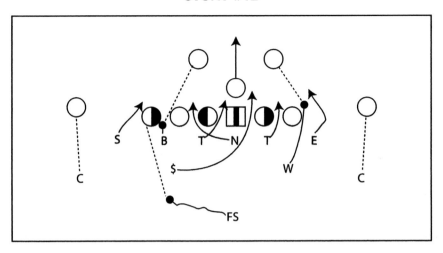

STUNT DESCRIPTION: This *illusion blitz* is enhanced by a strongside line twist.

SECONDARY COVERAGE: Zero coverage disguised as cover 1. Buck and Whip spy the running backs.

STUD: Rushes from the edge. Contains the quarterback and strongside run. Chases weakside run.

BUCK: Plays 7 technique versus run. Spies the near back versus pass.

STRONG SAFETY: Blitzes through the weakside A gap.

STRONG TACKLE: Slants to the A gap.

NOSE: Loops behind the left tackle into the B gap.

WEAK TACKLE: Slants to the B gap.

WEAK END: Slants outside. Contains the quarterback and weakside run. Chases strongside run.

WHIP: Attacks the outside shoulder of the offensive tackle. Secures the C gap versus run and spies the near back versus pass.

FREE SAFETY: Covers the tight end. Disguises his assignment as cover 1.

STRONG CORNER: Covers the flanker (inside technique).

WEAK CORNER: Covers the split end (inside technique).

STUNT #13

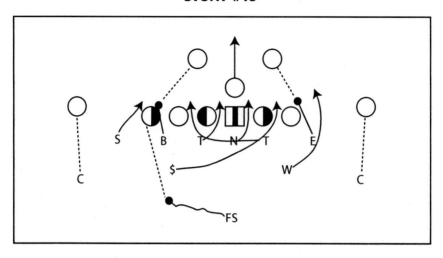

STUNT DESCRIPTION: This *illusion blitz* is enhanced by a strongside line twist.

SECONDARY COVERAGE: Zero coverage disguised as cover 1. Buck and the weak end spy the running backs.

STUD: Rushes from the edge. Contains the quarterback and strongside run. Chases weakside run.

BUCK: Plays 7 technique versus run. Spies the near back versus pass.

STRONG SAFETY: Blitzes through the weakside B gap.

STRONG TACKLE: Slants to the A gap.

NOSE: Slants to the weakside A gap.

WEAK TACKLE: Loops into the strongside B gap.

WEAK END: Attacks the near shoulder of the offensive tackle. Secures the C gap versus run and spies the near back versus pass.

WHIP: Scrapes outside. Contains the quarterback and weakside run. Chases strongside run.

FREE SAFETY: Covers the tight end. Disguises his assignment as cover 1.

STRONG CORNER: Covers the flanker (inside technique).

WEAK CORNER: Covers the split end (inside technique).

STUNT #14

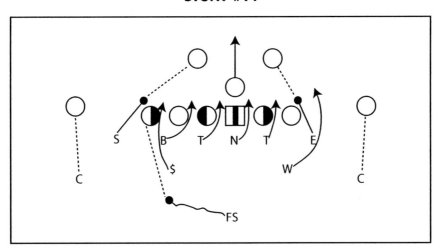

STUNT DESCRIPTION: This is an *illusion blitz.*

SECONDARY COVERAGE: Zero coverage disguised as cover 1. Stud and the weak end spy the running backs.

STUD: Comes across the line and gives the impression that he's rushing from the edge. Contains strongside run and chases weakside run. Spies the near back versus pass.

BUCK: Slants into the strongside B gap.

STRONG SAFETY: Blitzes through the inside shoulder of the tight end. Secures the C gap versus run and contains the quarterback versus pass.

STRONG TACKLE: Slants to the A gap.

NOSE: Slants to the weakside A gap.

WEAK TACKLE: Slants into the B gap.

WEAK END: Attacks the outside shoulder of the offensive tackle. Secures the C gap versus run and spies the near back versus pass.

WHIP: Scrapes outside. Contains the quarterback and weakside run. Chases strongside run.

FREE SAFETY: Covers the tight end. Disguises his assignment as cover 1.

STRONG CORNER: Covers the flanker (inside technique).

WEAK CORNER: Covers the split end (inside technique).

STUNT #15

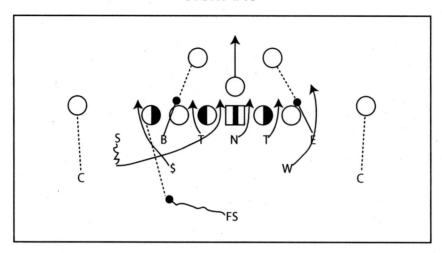

STUNT DESCRIPTION: This is an *illusion blitz*.

SECONDARY COVERAGE: Zero coverage disguised as cover 1. Buck and the weak end spy the running backs.

STUD: Sinks back during cadence and gives the impression that he intends to cover the tight end. Blitzes through the strongside A gap at the snap.

BUCK: Attacks the near shoulder of the offensive tackle. Secures the C gap versus run and spies the near back versus pass.

STRONG SAFETY: Scrapes to and attacks the outside shoulder of the tight end. Secures the D gap versus run and contains the quarterback versus pass.

STRONG TACKLE: Slants to the B gap.

NOSE: Slants to the weakside A gap.

WEAK TACKLE: Slants into the B gap.

WEAK END: Attacks the outside shoulder of the offensive tackle. Secures the C gap versus run and spies the near back versus pass.

WHIP: Scrapes outside. Contains the quarterback and weakside run. Chases strongside run.

FREE SAFETY: Covers the tight end. Disguises his assignment as cover 1.

STRONG CORNER: Covers the flanker (inside technique).

WEAK CORNER: Covers the split end (inside technique).

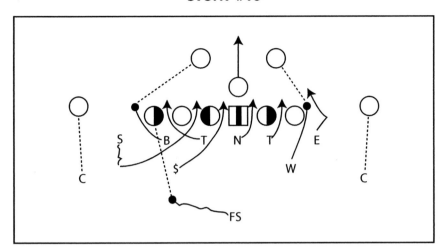

STUNT DESCRIPTION: This is an *illusion blitz*.

SECONDARY COVERAGE: Zero coverage disguised as cover 1. Buck and Whip spy the running backs.

STUD: Sinks back during cadence and gives the impression that he intends to cover the tight end. Blitzes through the strongside B gap at the snap.

BUCK: Slants across the tight end's face. Secures the D gap versus run and spies the near back versus pass.

STRONG SAFETY: Blitzes through the strongside A gap.

STRONG TACKLE: Slants across the offensive tackle's face and secures the strongside C gap versus run. Contains the quarterback versus pass.

NOSE: Slants to the weakside A gap.

WEAK TACKLE: Slants to the B gap.

WEAK END: Slants outside. Contains the quarterback and weakside run. Chases strongside run.

WHIP: Attacks the outside shoulder of the offensive tackle. Controls the C gap versus run and spies the near back versus pass.

FREE SAFETY: Covers the tight end. Disguises his assignment as cover 1.

STRONG CORNER: Covers the flanker (inside technique).

WEAK CORNER: Covers the split end (inside technique).

STUNT #17

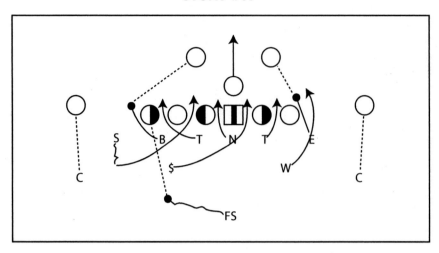

STUNT DESCRIPTION: This is an *illusion blitz*.

SECONDARY COVERAGE: Zero coverage disguised as cover 1. Buck and the weak end spy the running backs.

STUD: Sinks back during cadence and give the impression that he intends to cover the tight end. Blitzes through the strongside B gap at the snap.

BUCK: Slants across the tight end's face. Secures the D gap versus run and spies the near back versus pass.

STRONG SAFETY: Blitzes through the weakside A gap.

STRONG TACKLE: Slants across the offensive tackle's face and controls the C gap versus run. Contains the quarterback versus pass.

NOSE: Slants to the strongside A gap.

WEAK TACKLE: Slants to the B gap.

WEAK END: Attacks the near shoulder of the offensive tackle. Controls the C gap versus run and spies the near back versus pass.

WHIP: Scrapes outside. Contains the quarterback and weakside run. Chases strongside run.

FREE SAFETY: Covers the tight end. Disguises his assignment as cover 1.

STRONG CORNER: Covers the flanker (inside technique).

WEAK CORNER: Covers the split end (inside technique).

STUNT #18

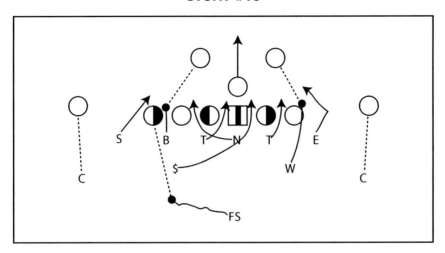

STUNT DESCRIPTION: This *illusion blitz* incorporates a line twist.

SECONDARY COVERAGE: Zero coverage disguised as cover 1. Buck and Whip spy the running backs.

STUD: Rushes from the edge. Contains the quarterback and strongside run. Chases weakside run.

BUCK: Plays 7 technique versus run. Spies the near back versus pass.

STRONG SAFETY: Blitzes through the weakside A gap.

STRONG TACKLE: Slants into the A gap.

NOSE: Loops behind the left tackle into the strongside B gap.

WEAK TACKLE: Slants to the B gap.

WEAK END: Slants outside. Contains the quarterback and weakside run. Chases strongside run.

WHIP: Attacks the outside shoulder of the offensive tackle. Controls the C gap versus run and spies the near back versus pass.

FREE SAFETY: Covers the tight end. Disguises his assignment as cover 1.

STRONG CORNER: Covers the flanker (inside technique).

WEAK CORNER: Covers the split end (inside technique).

STUNT #19

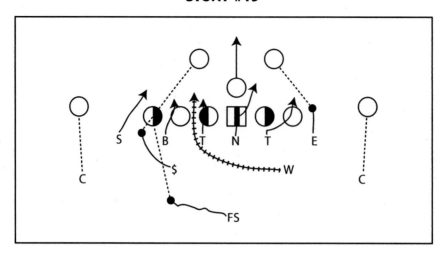

STUNT DESCRIPTION: This *delayed blitz* provides the defense with a strongside overload.

SECONDARY COVERAGE: Zero coverage disguised as cover 1. The strong safety and weak end spy the running backs.

STUD: Rushes from the edge. Contains the quarterback and strongside run. Chases weakside run.

BUCK: Attacks the near shoulder of the offensive tackle and controls the C gap.

STRONG SAFETY: Attacks the outside shoulder of the tight end and secures this area against run. Spies the near back versus pass.

STRONG TACKLE: Plays 3 technique.

NOSE: Plays 0 technique versus run. Slowly works his way into the weakside A gap versus pass.

WEAK TACKLE: Plays 3 technique versus run. Contain rushes versus pass.

WEAK END: Plays 7 technique versus run. Spies the near back versus pass.

WHIP: Plays base technique versus run. Delay rushes through the strongside B gap versus pass.

FREE SAFETY: Covers the tight end. Disguises his assignment as cover 1.

STRONG CORNER: Covers the flanker (inside technique).

WEAK CORNER: Covers the split end (inside technique).

STUNT #20

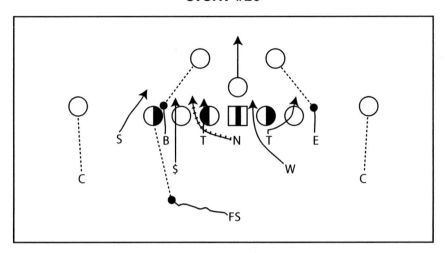

STUNT DESCRIPTION: This blitz incorporates a *delayed line twist* (twin stunt) that provides the defense with a strongside overload.

SECONDARY COVERAGE: Zero coverage disguised as cover 1. Buck and the weak end spy the running backs.

STUD: Rushes from the edge. Contains the quarterback and strongside run. Chases weakside run.

BUCK: Plays 7 technique versus run. Spies the near back versus pass.

STRONG SAFETY: Blitzes through the outside shoulder of the offensive tackle and controls the C gap.

STRONG TACKLE: Plays 3 technique.

NOSE: Plays 0 technique versus run. Loops into the strongside B gap versus pass.

WEAK TACKLE: Plays 3 technique versus run. Contain rushes versus pass.

WEAK END: Plays 7 technique versus run. Spies the near back versus pass.

WHIP: Blitzes through the weakside A gap.

FREE SAFETY: Covers the tight end. Disguises his assignment as cover 1.

STRONG CORNER: Covers the flanker (inside technique).

WEAK CORNER: Covers the split end (inside technique).

STUNT #21

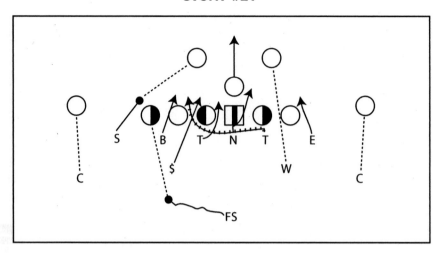

STUNT DESCRIPTION: This blitz features a *delayed line twist* (twin stunt) that provides the defense with a strongside overload.

SECONDARY COVERAGE: Zero coverage disguised as cover 1. Stud and Whip spy the running backs.

STUD: Rushes from the edge. Contains strongside run and chases weakside run. Spies the near back versus pass.

BUCK: Attacks the near shoulder of the offensive tackle. Controls the C gap versus run and contains the quarterback versus pass.

STRONG SAFETY: Attacks the outside shoulder of the offensive guard and secures the B gap.

STRONG TACKLE: Slants into the A gap.

NOSE: Plays 0 technique versus run. Slowly works his way into the weakside A gap versus pass.

WEAK TACKLE: Plays 3 technique versus run. Loops into the strongside B gap (twin stunt) versus pass.

WEAK END: Plays 7 technique versus run. Contains the quarterback versus pass.

WHIP: Plays base technique versus run. Covers the near back versus pass.

FREE SAFETY: Covers the tight end. Disguises his assignment as cover 1.

STRONG CORNER: Covers the flanker (inside technique).

WEAK CORNER: Covers the split end (inside technique).

STUNT #22

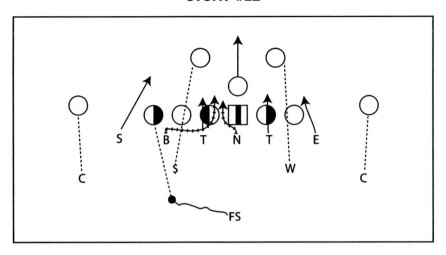

STUNT DESCRIPTION: This blitz features a *delayed blitz* (twin stunt) by Buck that provides the defense with a strongside overload.

SECONDARY COVERAGE: Zero coverage disguised as cover 1. The strong safety and Whip spy the running backs.

STUD: Rushes from the edge. Contains the quarterback and strongside run. Chases weakside run.

BUCK: Plays 7 technique versus run. Delay rushes (twin stunt) through the A gap versus pass.

STRONG SAFETY: Plays base technique versus run. Covers the near back versus pass.

STRONG TACKLE: Plays 3 technique.

NOSE: Plays 0 technique versus run. Slants into the strongside A gap versus pass.

WEAK TACKLE: Plays 3 technique.

WEAK END: Plays 7 technique versus run. Contains the quarterback versus pass.

WHIP: Plays base technique versus run. Covers the near back versus pass.

FREE SAFETY: Covers the tight end. Disguises his assignment as cover 1.

STRONG CORNER: Covers the flanker (inside technique).

WEAK CORNER: Covers the split end (inside technique).

STUNT #23

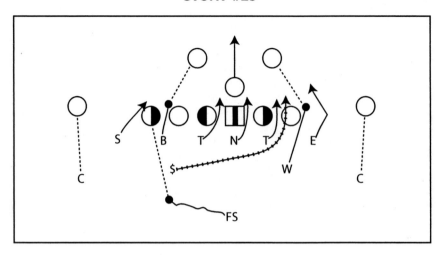

STUNT DESCRIPTION: This blitz features a *delayed blitz* by the strong safety that provides the defense with a weakside overload.

SECONDARY COVERAGE: Zero coverage disguised as cover 1. Buck and Whip spy the running backs.

STUD: Rushes from the edge. Contains the quarterback and strongside run. Chases weakside run.

BUCK: Attacks the near shoulder of the offensive tackle and secures the C gap versus run. Spies the near back versus pass.

STRONG SAFETY: Plays base technique versus run.Delay blitzes (twin stunt) through the weakside B gap versus pass.

STRONG TACKLE: Slants into the A gap.

NOSE: Slants into the weakside A gap.

WEAK TACKLE: Slants into the B gap.

WEAK END: Slants outside and secures the D gap versus run. Contains the quarterback versus pass.

WHIP: Attacks the outside shoulder of the offensive tackle. Secures the C gap versus run and spies the near back versus pass.

FREE SAFETY: Covers the tight end. Disguises his assignment as cover 1.

STRONG CORNER: Covers the flanker (inside technique).

WEAK CORNER: Covers the split end (inside technique).

STUNT #24

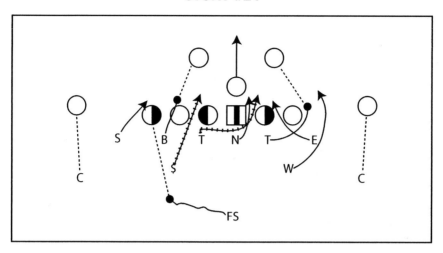

STUNT DESCRIPTION: This blitz incorporates both a *delayed line twist* and *delayed linebacker blitz* that provides the defense with a weakside overload.

SECONDARY COVERAGE: Zero coverage disguised as cover 1. Buck and the weak tackle spy the running backs.

STUD: Rushes from the edge. Contains the quarterback and strongside run. Chases weakside run.

BUCK: Attacks the near shoulder of the offensive tackle and secures the C gap versus run. Spies the near back versus pass.

STRONG SAFETY: Plays base technique versus run. Delay blitzes through the strongside B gap versus pass.

STRONG TACKLE: Plays 3 technique versus run. Loops into the weakside A gap (twin stunt) versus pass.

NOSE: Slants into the weakside A gap.

WEAK TACKLE: Loops behind the weak end through the outside shoulder of the offensive tackle. Secures the C gap versus run and spies the near back versus pass.

WEAK END: Slants into the B gap.

WHIP: Blitzes into the D gap. Contains the quarterback and weakside run. Chases strongside run.

FREE SAFETY: Covers the tight end. Disguises his assignment as cover 1.

STRONG CORNER: Covers the flanker (inside technique).

WEAK CORNER: Covers the split end (inside technique).

STUNT #25

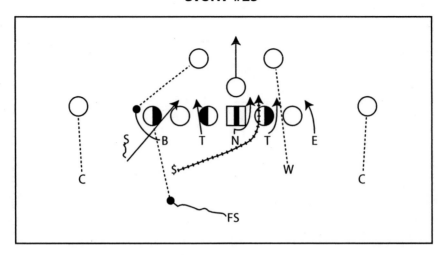

STUNT DESCRIPTION: This *delayed blitz* by the strong safety provides the defense with a weakside overload.

SECONDARY COVERAGE: Zero coverage disguised as cover 1. Buck and Whip spy the running backs.

STUD: Sinks back during cadence and gives the impression that he's covering the tight end. Blitzes through the C gap at the snap.

BUCK: Slants across the tight end's face and secures the D gap versus run. Spies the near back versus pass.

STRONG SAFETY: Plays base technique versus run. Delay blitzes (twin stunt) through the weakside A gap versus pass.

STRONG TACKLE: Plays 3 technique.

NOSE: Plays 0 technique versus run. Slants into the weakside A gap versus pass.

WEAK TACKLE: Plays 3 technique.

WEAK END: Plays 7 technique versus run. Contains the quarterback versus pass.

WHIP: Plays base technique versus run. Covers the near back versus pass.

FREE SAFETY: Covers the tight end. Disguises his assignment as cover 1.

STRONG CORNER: Covers the flanker (inside technique).

WEAK CORNER: Covers the split end (inside technique).

STUNT #26

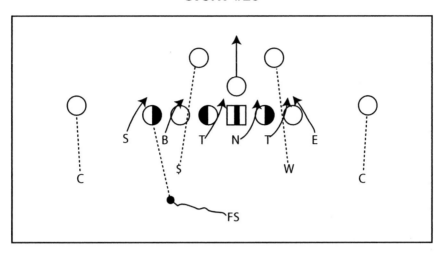

STUNT DESCRIPTION: This blitz provides the defense with a weakside line slant.

SECONDARY COVERAGE: Zero coverage disguised as cover 1. The strong safety and Whip cover the running backs.

STUD: Rushes from the edge. Contains the quarterback and strongside run. Chases weakside run.

BUCK: Attacks the near shoulder of the offensive tackle and controls the C gap.

STRONG SAFETY: Secures the B gap versus strongside run. Pursues weakside run from an inside-out position and covers the near back versus pass.

STRONG TACKLE: Slants into the A gap.

NOSE: Slants into the weakside A gap.

WEAK TACKLE: Slants into the B gap.

WEAK END: Controls the C gap versus run. Contains the quarterback versus pass.

WHIP: Scrapes outside and contains the weakside run. Pursues strongside run from an inside-out position. Covers the near back versus pass.

FREE SAFETY: Covers the tight end. Disguises his assignment as cover 1.

STRONG CORNER: Covers the flanker (inside technique).

WEAK CORNER: Covers the split end (inside technique).

STUNT #27

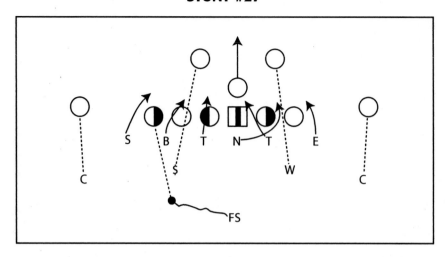

STUNT DESCRIPTION: This blitz provides the defense with a weakside line twist.

SECONDARY COVERAGE: Zero coverage disguised as cover 1. The strong safety and Whip cover the running backs.

STUD: Rushes from the edge. Contains the quarterback and strongside run. Chases weakside run.

BUCK: Attacks the near shoulder of the offensive tackle and controls the C gap.

STRONG SAFETY: Plays base technique versus run and covers the near back versus pass.

STRONG TACKLE: Plays 3 technique.

NOSE: Loops behind the right tackle into the weakside B gap.

WEAK TACKLE: Slants into the A gap.

WEAK END: Secures the C gap versus run. Contains the quarterback versus pass.

WHIP: Scrapes outside and contains the weakside run. Pursues strongside run from an inside-out position. Covers the near back versus pass.

FREE SAFETY: Covers the tight end. Disguises his assignment as cover 1.

STRONG CORNER: Covers the flanker (inside technique).

WEAK CORNER: Covers the split end (inside technique).

STUNT #28

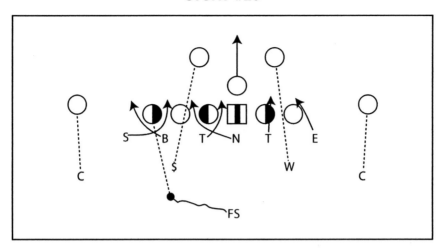

STUNT DESCRIPTION: This blitz provides the defense with a strongside line twist.

SECONDARY COVERAGE: Zero coverage disguised as cover 1. The strong safety and Whip cover the running backs.

STUD: Loops behind Buck into the C gap.

BUCK: Slants outside and secures the D gap versus run. Contains the quarterback versus pass.

STRONG SAFETY: Plays base technique versus run. Covers the near back versus pass.

STRONG TACKLE: Slants into the A gap.

NOSE: Loops behind the left tackle into the strongside B gap.

WEAK TACKLE: Plays 3 technique.

WEAK END: Secures the C gap versus run. Contains the quarterback versus pass.

WHIP: Scrapes outside and contains the weakside run. Pursues strongside run from an inside-out position. Covers the near back versus pass.

FREE SAFETY: Covers the tight end. Disguises his assignment as cover 1.

STRONG CORNER: Covers the flanker (inside technique).

WEAK CORNER: Covers the split end (inside technique).

STUNT #29

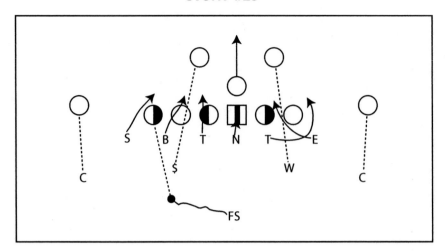

STUNT DESCRIPTION: This blitz provides the defense with a weakside line twist.

SECONDARY COVERAGE: Zero coverage disguised as cover 1. The strong safety and Whip cover the running backs.

STUD: Rushes from the edge. Contains the quarterback and strongside run. Chases weakside run.

BUCK: Attacks the near shoulder of the offensive tackle and controls the C gap.

STRONG SAFETY: Plays base technique versus run and covers the near back versus pass.

STRONG TACKLE: Plays 3 technique.

NOSE: Plays 0 technique.

WEAK TACKLE: Loops behind the weak end. Secures the C gap versus run and contains the quarterback versus pass.

WEAK END: Slants into the B gap.

WHIP: Scrapes outside and contains the weakside run. Pursues strongside run from an inside-out position. Covers the near back versus pass.

FREE SAFETY: Covers the tight end. Disguises his assignment as cover 1.

STRONG CORNER: Covers the flanker (inside technique).

WEAK CORNER: Covers the split end (inside technique).

STUNT #30

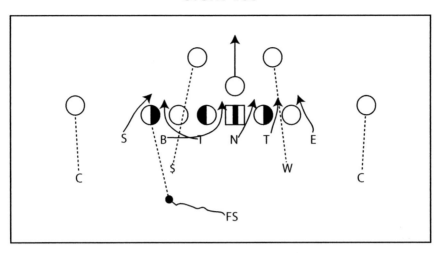

STUNT DESCRIPTION: This blitz provides the defense with both a weakside line slant and a twist between Buck and the strong tackle.

SECONDARY COVERAGE: Zero coverage disguised as cover 1. The strong safety and Whip cover the running backs.

STUD: Rushes from the edge. Contains the quarterback and strongside run. Chases weakside run.

BUCK: Loops behind the strong tackle into the strongside A gap.

STRONG SAFETY: Plays base technique versus run. Covers the near back versus pass.

STRONG TACKLE: Slants to the far shoulder of the offensive tackle and secures the strongside C gap.

NOSE: Slants into the weakside A gap.

WEAK TACKLE: Slants into the B gap.

WEAK END: Secures the C gap versus run. Contains the quarterback versus pass.

WHIP: Scrapes outside and contains the weakside run. Pursues strongside run from an inside-out position. Covers the near back versus pass.

FREE SAFETY: Covers the tight end. Disguises his assignment as cover 1.

STRONG CORNER: Covers the flanker (inside technique).

WEAK CORNER: Covers the split end (inside technique).

STUNT #31

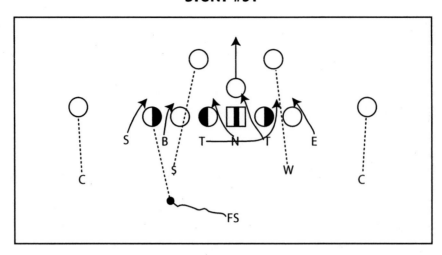

STUNT DESCRIPTION: This blitz provides the defense with an inside line twist.

SECONDARY COVERAGE: Zero coverage disguised as cover 1. The strong safety and Whip cover the running backs.

STUD: Rushes from the edge. Contains the quarterback and strongside run. Chases weakside run.

BUCK: Attacks the near shoulder of the offensive tackle and controls the C gap.

STRONG SAFETY: Secures the B gap versus strongside run. Pursues weakside run from an inside-out position and covers the near back versus pass.

STRONG TACKLE: Loops to the outside shoulder of the offensive guard and secures the weakside B gap.

NOSE: Slants into the strongside A gap.

WEAK TACKLE: Slants into the A gap.

WEAK END: Secures the C gap versus run. Contains the quarterback versus pass.

WHIP: Scrapes outside and contains the weakside run. Pursues strongside run from an inside-out position. Covers the near back versus pass.

FREE SAFETY: Covers the tight end. Disguises his assignment as cover 1.

STRONG CORNER: Covers the flanker (inside technique).

WEAK CORNER: Covers the split end (inside technique).

STUNT #32

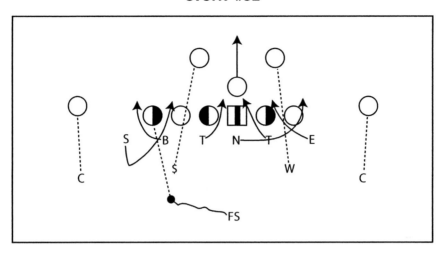

STUNT DESCRIPTION: This blitz provides the defense with a weakside line twist and a twist between Stud and Buck.

SECONDARY COVERAGE: Zero coverage disguised as cover 1. The strong safety and Whip cover the running backs.

STUD: Sinks back as though he intends to cover the tight end and then blitzes through the strongside C gap.

BUCK: Slants outside. Controls the D gap versus run and contains the quarterback versus pass.

STRONG SAFETY: Secures the B gap versus strongside run. Pursues weakside run from an inside-out position and covers the near back versus pass.

STRONG TACKLE: Slants into the A gap.

NOSE: Loops to the outside shoulder of the offensive tackle and secures the weakside C gap versus run. Contains the quarterback versus pass.

WEAK TACKLE: Slants into the A gap.

WEAK END: Slants into the B gap.

WHIP: Scrapes outside and contains the weakside run. Pursues strongside run from an inside-out position. Covers the near back versus pass.

FREE SAFETY: Covers the tight end. Disguises his assignment as cover 1.

STRONG CORNER: Covers the flanker (inside technique).

WEAK CORNER: Covers the split end (inside technique).

STUNT #33

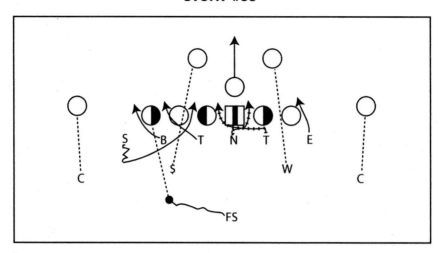

STUNT DESCRIPTION: This blitz provides the defense with excellent strongside run support and a delayed line twist versus pass.

SECONDARY COVERAGE: Zero coverage disguised as cover 1. The strong safety and Whip cover the running backs.

STUD: Sinks back as though he intends to cover the tight end and then blitzes through the strongside B gap.

BUCK: Slants outside. Controls the D gap versus run and contains the quarterback versus pass.

STRONG SAFETY: Scrapes outside and assists in containment versus strongside run. Pursues weakside run from an inside-out position and covers the near back versus pass.

STRONG TACKLE: Slants to the far shoulder of the offensive tackle and secures the strongside C gap.

NOSE: Plays 0 technique versus run. Slants into the weakside A gap versus pass.

WEAK TACKLE: Plays 3 technique versus run. Loops behind the nose into the strongside A gap versus pass.

WEAK END: Secures the C gap versus weakside run and chases strongside run. Contains the quarterback versus pass.

WHIP: Scrapes outside and contains the weakside run. Pursues strongside run from an inside-out position. Covers the near back versus pass.

FREE SAFETY: Covers the tight end. Disguises his assignment as cover 1.

STRONG CORNER: Covers the flanker (inside technique).

WEAK CORNER: Covers the split end (inside technique).

STUNT #34

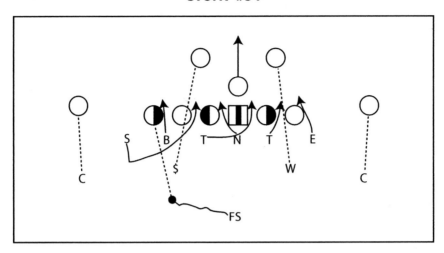

STUNT DESCRIPTION: This blitz sends Buck and Stud, features a line twist, and provides the defense with excellent weakside run support.

SECONDARY COVERAGE: Zero coverage disguised as cover 1. The strong safety and Whip cover the running backs.

STUD: Sinks back as though he intends to cover the tight end and then blitzes through the strongside B gap.

BUCK: Plays 7 technique versus run. Contains the quarterback versus pass.

STRONG SAFETY: Scrapes outside and contains the strongside run. Pursues weakside run from an inside-out position. Covers the near back versus pass.

STRONG TACKLE: Loops behind the nose into the weakside A gap.

NOSE: Slants into the strongside A gap.

WEAK TACKLE: Slants into the B gap.

WEAK END: Secures the C gap versus weakside run and chases strongside run. Contains the quarterback versus pass.

WHIP: Scrapes outside and contains the weakside run. Pursues strongside run from an inside-out position. Covers the near back versus pass.

FREE SAFETY: Covers the tight end. Disguises his assignment as cover 1.

STRONG CORNER: Covers the flanker (inside technique).

WEAK CORNER: Covers the split end (inside technique).

STUNT #35

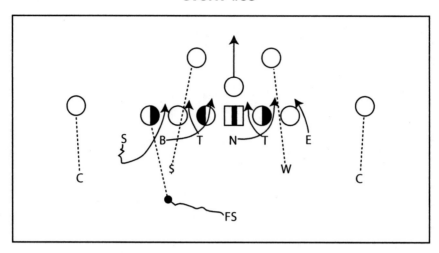

STUNT DESCRIPTION: This blitz sends Buck and Stud and provides the defense with a weakside line twist.

SECONDARY COVERAGE: Zero coverage disguised as cover 1. The strong safety and Whip cover the running backs.

STUD: Sinks back as though he intends to cover the tight end and then blitzes through the strongside C gap.

BUCK: Loops behind the strong tackle into the strongside A gap.

STRONG SAFETY: Scrapes outside and contains the strongside run. Pursues weakside run from an inside-out position. Covers the near back versus pass.

STRONG TACKLE: Quickly penetrates the B gap.

NOSE: Loops behind the weak tackle into the weakside B gap.

WEAK TACKLE: Quickly slants into the A gap.

WEAK END: Secures the C gap versus weakside run and chases strongside run. Contains the quarterback versus pass.

WHIP: Scrapes outside and contain the weakside run. Pursues strongside run from an inside-out position. Covers the near back versus pass.

FREE SAFETY: Covers the tight end. Disguises his assignment as cover 1.

STRONG CORNER: Covers the flanker (inside technique).

WEAK CORNER: Covers the split end (inside technique).

STUNT #36

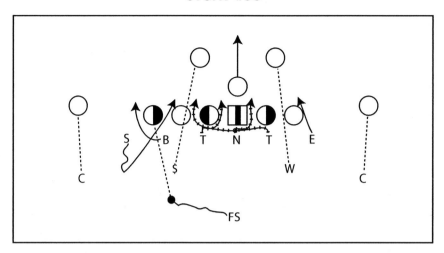

STUNT DESCRIPTION: This blitz sends Buck and Stud and provides the defense with a delayed line twist versus pass.

SECONDARY COVERAGE: Zero coverage disguised as cover 1. The strong safety and Whip cover the running backs.

STUD: Sinks back as though he intends to cover the tight end and then blitzes through the strongside C gap.

BUCK: Slants outside. Controls the D gap versus run and contains the quarterback versus pass.

STRONG SAFETY: Scrapes outside and assists in containment versus strongside run. Pursues weakside run from an inside-out position and covers the near back versus pass.

STRONG TACKLE: Plays 3 technique versus run. Quickly penetrates the A gap versus pass.

NOSE: Plays 0 technique versus run. Quickly penetrates the weakside A gap versus pass.

WEAK TACKLE: Plays 3 technique versus run. Loops into the strongside B gap versus pass.

WEAK END: Secures the C gap versus weakside run and chases strongside run. Contains the quarterback versus pass.

WHIP: Scrapes outside and contains the weakside run. Pursues strongside run from an inside-out position. Covers the near back versus pass.

FREE SAFETY: Covers the tight end. Disguises his assignment as cover 1.

STRONG CORNER: Covers the flanker (inside technique).

WEAK CORNER: Covers the split end (inside technique).

CHAPTER 4

Cover 1 Stunts

Cover 1 is a man-to-man coverage with the free safety free. The strength of this coverage is that the free safety is keying the ball, playing center field, and backing up the two cornerbacks and the eight defenders in the box. Another strength of this coverage is that it is a man-to-man coverage and the offense cannot high-low zones or attack seams. An additional strength with this coverage is that the cornerbacks can use bump, trail, or loose-man techniques, and easily disguise which technique they are using. This not only inhibits the quarterback's pre-snap read, but when the bump technique is employed, it disrupts the timing of the receivers' routes.

Despite the advantages of playing cover 1, cover 1 stunts do not exert as much pressure on the offense as zero coverage stunts. This weakness can be somewhat offset by incorporating *illusion dogs*, *fire zone blitzes*, and *hybrid fire zone blitzes* into the stunt package.

Whom Can the Free Safety Help?

Although cover 1 employs a free safety, the two cornerbacks can't realistically count on the free safety to assist them with all deep patterns. The field is simply too wide to expect the free safety to cover the entire area between the two sidelines. When a cornerback can expect inside help from the free safety, he should employ an outside-leverage technique. When a cornerback can't expect inside help, he should employ an inside-leverage technique. Figures 4-1a through 4-1c show three common formation strength/field position situations that will determine the cornerback's leverage technique.

In Figure 4-1a, the strong cornerback cannot expect to receive inside help. He should therefore maintain inside leverage on the flanker. Although the weak cornerback could receive help from the free safety, he should employ an inside leverage technique and take away the split end's inside routes because the split end is close to the sideline and it is doubtful that he will attempt to run outside routes.

Because both receivers in Figure 4-1b have assumed tight splits, both cornerbacks can expect to receive inside help and should maintain outside leverage. Although the ball is in the middle of the field in Figure 4-1c, both the flanker and the split end have assumed wide splits. The two cornerbacks should therefore maintain inside leverage because it is doubtful that the safety can help either of them with inside routes.

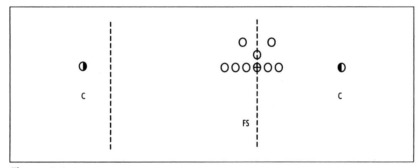

Figure 4-1a

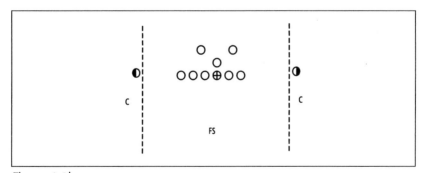

Figure 4-1b

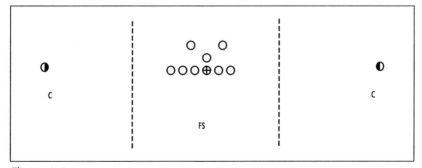

Figure 4-1c

Techniques and Assignments for Fire Zone Blitz Drops

The fire zone blitz has become an extremely popular stunt tactic in recent years. As noted in Chapter One, when a fire zone blitz is employed, three defenders drop into the under coverage and share the joint responsibility of combo-covering the tight end and the two running backs. We refer to the under coverage drops as **Abel**, **Baker**, and **Charlie**. The techniques and assignments for these drops are as follows:

Assignments and Techniques for Abel's Drop:

- **Abel** drops to a position that will enable him to attain outside leverage on #2.

- Keys #2 to #3.

- If #2 runs a quick out (six yards or less), the defender immediately jumps his pattern and establishes a 3-yard cushion (Figure 4-2).

- If #2 runs a vertical route and #3 runs an out pattern of six yards or less, the defender gains depth and squeezes #2 inside. He should not be in a big hurry to jump #3's out pattern because #2 may turn his vertical route into a deep out. The defender relinquishes his cushion on #2 and tries to work to a depth of 8 to 10 yards. As #3 starts to cross **Abel's** face, the defender begins to widen and establishes a loose cushion on #3, but tries to stay in the throwing lane between the quarterback and #2 for as long as possible. **Baker** will help by alerting **Abel** with an "out-out" call in the event that #2 does turn his vertical route into a deep out (Figure 4-3).

- If #2 runs a vertical route and #3 either blocks or runs a short inside route, **Abel** locks on to #2, squeezes him inside, maintains outside leverage, and forces him to run a collision course (Figure 4-4).

- If #2 runs a quick crossing pattern, the defender keys #3 to #4 (Figure 4-5).

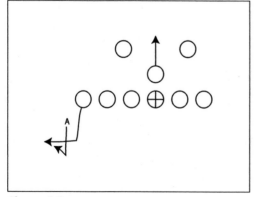

Figure 4-2

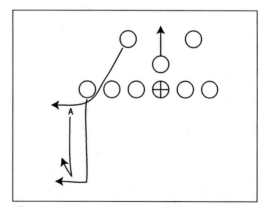

Figure 4-3

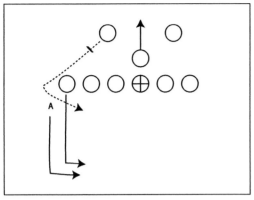

Figure 4-4

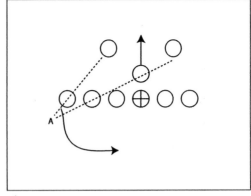

Figure 4-5

Assignments and Techniques for Baker's Drop:

- **Baker** drops to a position that enables him to establish inside leverage on #2, but keeps #3 in his periphery.

- Keys #2 to #3.

- If #2 runs a vertical route, **Baker** gains depth and covers him from an inside-out position, keeping #3 in his periphery. If #3 blocks or runs a short out pattern, the defender locks on to #2 (Figure 4-6a). If #3 runs a short in pattern, **Baker** releases his coverage of #2 and locks on to #3 (Figure 4-6b).

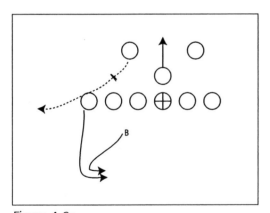

Figure 4-6a

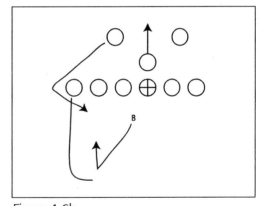

Figure 4-6b

- If #2 runs a quick crossing pattern (six yards or less), **Baker** immediately calls "in-in", jams #2, walls him off, and forces him to deepen his pattern. The defender then locks on to #2 (Figure4-7a) unless **Charlie** echoes **Baker's** "in-in" call. If **Charlie** echoes **Baker's** call, it is because #2 and #4 are crossing. If #2 and #4 cross, **Baker** releases his coverage of #2, gains depth, and locks on to #4 (Figure 4-7b).

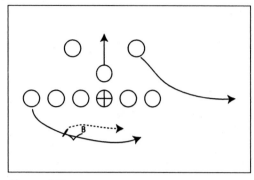

Figure 4-7a

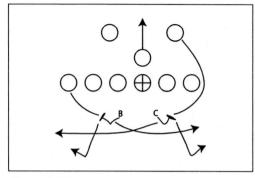

Figure 4-7b

- If #2 runs a quick out pattern, **Baker** immediately redirects his attention to #3 and covers him (Figure 4-8a). If #3 and #4 try to run short crossing patterns, **Baker** follows the same rules as when #2 and #4 ran short crossing patterns (Figure 4-8b).

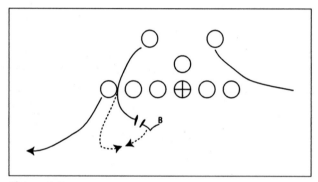

Figure 4-8a

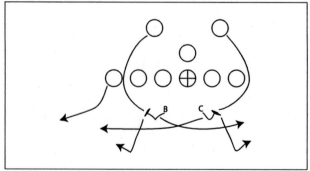

Figure 4-8b

Assignments and Techniques for Charlie's Drop:

- **Charlie** opens up and drops to a position that will enable him to cover #4 from an inside-out position.

- Key #4 but stays alert for an "in-in" call from **Baker.**

- If #4 runs a quick crossing pattern (six yards or less), **Charlie** immediately jams #4, walls him off, and forces him to deepen his pattern. **Charlie** locks on to #4 (Figure 4-9a) unless **Baker** has given an "in-in" call (**Baker** will be the first one to give the call because #2 is aligned on the line of scrimmage and #4 is in the backfield). If **Baker** calls "in-in", **Charlie** echoes his call, releases his coverage of #4, gains depth, and locks on to #2 or #3 (Figure 4-9b).

- **Charlie** covers #4 on all other routes.

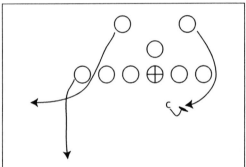

Figure 4-9a   Figure 4-9b

Fire Zone Coverage Versus the *Dirty Dozen*

Figures 4-10a through 4-10l show how the fire zone would adjust to and cover 12 of the toughest patterns it will ever face.

Hybrid Fire Zone Coverage

Hybrid fire zone coverage is very similar to fire zone coverage. There are two main differences between the two. First, hybrid fire zone coverage assigns only two defenders to drop into the under coverage. These two players drop **Abel/Baker** and combo-cover the tight end and the strongside halfback. Secondly, an illusion stunt will be employed on the weakside and one of the defenders involved in that stunt will be assigned to "spy" the weakside halfback. Figures 4-11a through l show how hybrid fire zone coverage functions versus the "dirty dozen" (the symbol X is used to designate the weakside defender who is assigned to "spy" the weakside halfback.

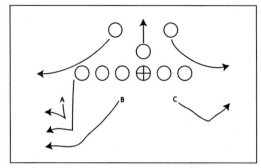

Figure 4-10a

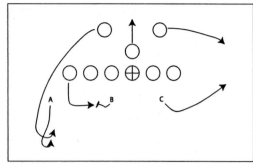

Figure 4-10b

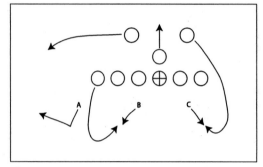

Figure 4-10c

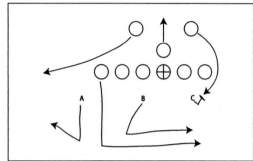

Figure 4-10d

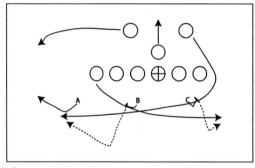

Figure 4-10e

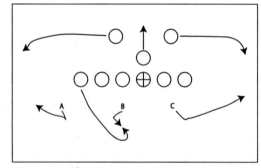

Figure 4-10f

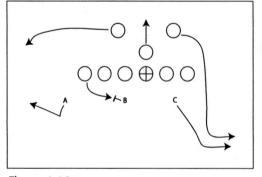

Figure 4-10g

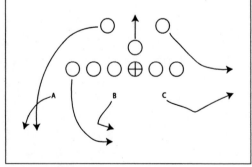

Figure 4-10h

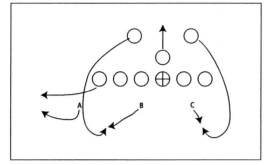

Figure 4-10i

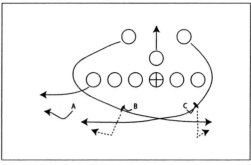

Figure 4-10j

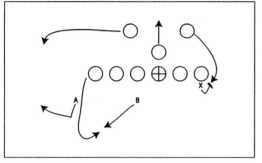

Figure 4-10k

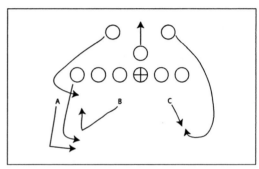

Figure 4-10l

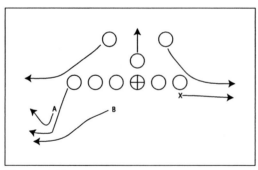

Figure 4-11a

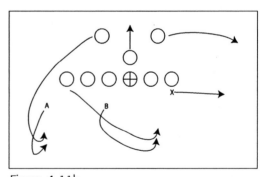

Figure 4-11b

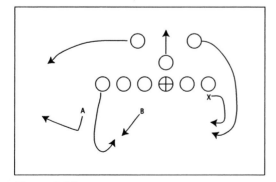

Figure 4-11c

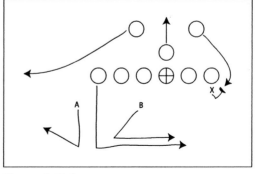

Figure 4-11d

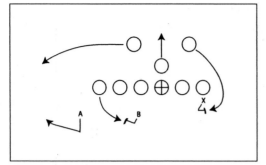

Figure 4-11e

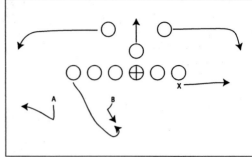

Figure 4-11f

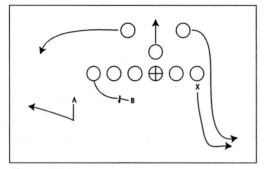

Figure 4-11g

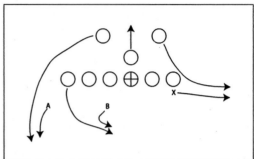

Figure 4-11h

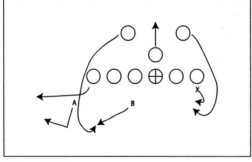

Figure 4-11i

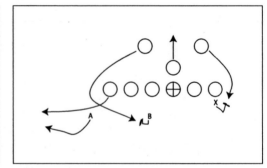

Figure 4-11j

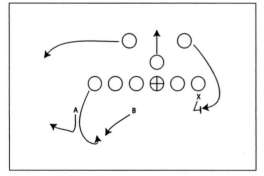

Figure 4-11k

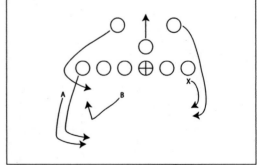

Figure 4-11l

STUNT #37

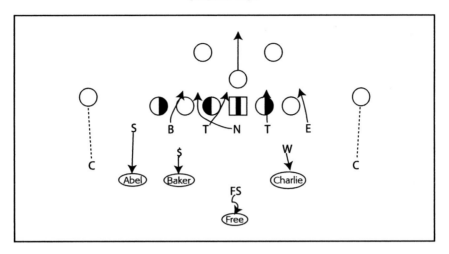

STUNT DESCRIPTION: This *fire zone blitz* sends Buck and provides the defense with a strongside line twist.

SECONDARY COVERAGE: Cover 1. The strong safety, Stud, and Whip drop into coverage and the free safety plays center field.

STUD: Plays 8 technique versus run. Drops **Abel** versus pass.

BUCK: Slants into the near shoulder of the offensive tackle and secures the C gap versus run. Contains the quarterback versus pass.

STRONG SAFETY: Plays base technique versus run. Drops **Baker** versus pass.

STRONG TACKLE: Slants across the face of the offensive guard into the A gap.

NOSE: Loops behind the slanting tackle into the strongside B gap.

WEAK TACKLE: Plays 3 technique.

WEAK END: Plays 7 technique versus run. Contains the quarterback versus pass.

WHIP: Plays base technique versus run. Drops **Charlie** versus pass.

FREE SAFETY: Lines up as though he's playing cover 3. Provides alley support versus run. Plays center field versus pass.

STRONG CORNER: Covers receiver #1 (inside/outside technique dependent upon field position and the distance of the flanker's split).

WEAK CORNER: Covers receiver #1 (inside/outside technique dependent upon field position and the distance of the split end's split).

STUNT #38

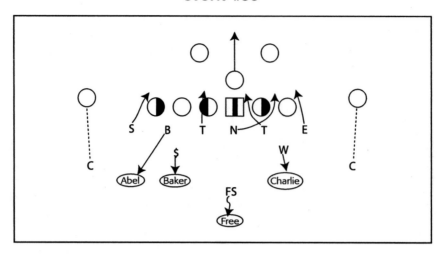

STUNT DESCRIPTION: This *fire zone blitz* sends Stud and provides the defense with a weakside line twist.

SECONDARY COVERAGE: Cover 1. The strong safety, Buck, and Whip drop into coverage and the free safety plays center field.

STUD: Rushes from the edge. Contains the quarterback and strongside run. Chases weakside run.

BUCK: Plays 7 technique versus run. Drops **Abel** versus pass.

STRONG SAFETY: Plays base technique versus run. Drops **Baker** versus pass.

STRONG TACKLE: Plays 3 technique.

NOSE: Loops behind the slanting tackle into the weakside B gap.

WEAK TACKLE: Slants across the face of the offensive guard into the A gap.

WEAK END: Plays 7 technique versus run. Contains the quarterback versus pass.

WHIP: Plays base technique versus run. Drops **Charlie** versus pass.

FREE SAFETY: Lines up as though he's playing cover 3. Provides alley support versus run. Plays center field versus pass.

STRONG CORNER: Covers receiver #1 (inside/outside technique dependent upon field position and the distance of the flanker's split).

WEAK CORNER: Covers receiver #1 (inside/outside technique dependent upon field position and the distance of the split end's split).

STUNT #39

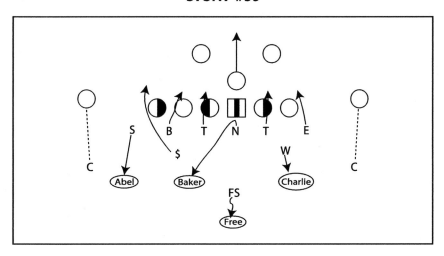

STUNT DESCRIPTION: This *fire zone blitz* sends both Buck and the strong safety.

SECONDARY COVERAGE: Cover 1. Stud, nose, and Whip drop into coverage and the free safety plays center field.

STUD: Plays 8 technique versus run. Drops **Abel** versus pass.

BUCK: Attacks the near shoulder of the offensive tackle and secures the C gap.

STRONG SAFETY: Blitzes through the outside shoulder of the tight end. Secures the D gap and contains the quarterback.

STRONG TACKLE: Plays 3 technique.

NOSE: Plays 0 technique versus run. Drops **Baker** versus pass.

WEAK TACKLE: Plays 3 technique.

WEAK END: Plays 7 technique versus run. Contains the quarterback versus pass.

WHIP: Plays base technique versus run. Drops **Charlie** versus pass.

FREE SAFETY: Lines up as though he's playing cover 3. Provides alley support versus run. Plays center field versus pass.

STRONG CORNER: Covers receiver #1 (inside/outside technique dependent upon field position and the distance of the flanker's split).

WEAK CORNER: Covers receiver #1 (inside/outside technique dependent upon field position and the distance of the split end's split).

STUNT #40

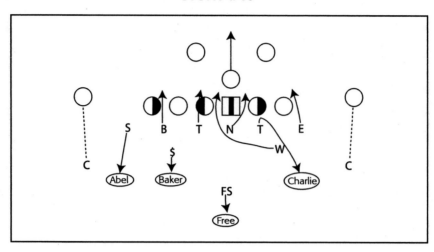

STUNT DESCRIPTION: This *fire zone blitz* sends Whip and Buck.

SECONDARY COVERAGE: Cover 1. The strong safety, Stud, and the weak tackle drop into coverage and the free safety plays center field.

STUD: Plays 8 technique versus run. Drops **Abel** versus pass.

BUCK: Plays 7 technique versus run. Contains the quarterback versus pass.

STRONG SAFETY: Plays base technique versus run. Drops **Baker** versus pass.

STRONG TACKLE: Plays 3 technique.

NOSE: Slants into the weakside A gap.

WEAK TACKLE: Plays 3 technique versus run. Drops **Charlie** versus pass.

WEAK END: Plays 7 technique versus run. Contains the quarterback versus pass.

WHIP: Blitzes through the strongside A gap.

FREE SAFETY: Lines up as though he's playing cover 3. Provides alley support versus run. Plays center field versus pass.

STRONG CORNER: Covers receiver #1 (inside/outside technique dependent upon field position and the distance of the flanker's split).

WEAK CORNER: Covers receiver #1 (inside/outside technique dependent upon field position and the distance of the split end's split).

STUNT #41

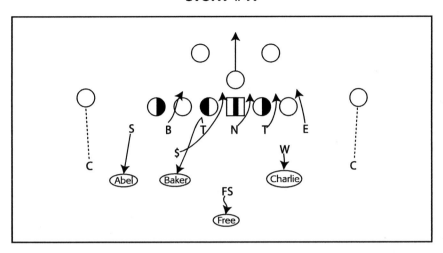

STUNT DESCRIPTION: This *fire zone blitz* sends the strong safety and Buck.

SECONDARY COVERAGE: Cover 1. Stud, Whip, and the strong tackle drop into coverage and the free safety plays center field.

STUD: Plays 8 technique versus run. Drops **Abel** versus pass.

BUCK: Slants to the near shoulder of the offensive tackle. Secures the C gap and contains the quarterback.

STRONG SAFETY: Blitzes through the strongside A gap.

STRONG TACKLE: Plays 3 technique versus run. Drops **Baker** versus pass.

NOSE: Slants into the weakside A gap.

WEAK TACKLE: Slants into the B gap

WEAK END: Plays 7 technique versus run. Contains the quarterback versus pass.

WHIP: Plays base technique versus run. Drops **Charlie** versus pass.

FREE SAFETY: Lines up as though he's playing cover 3. Provides alley support versus run. Plays center field versus pass.

STRONG CORNER: Covers receiver #1 (inside/outside technique dependent upon field position and the distance of the flanker's split).

WEAK CORNER: Covers receiver #1 (inside/outside technique dependent upon field position and the distance of the split end's split).

STUNT #42

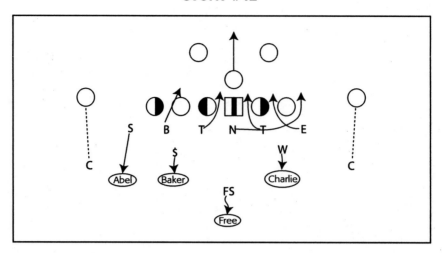

STUNT DESCRIPTION: This *fire zone blitz* sends Buck and provides the defense with a weakside line twist.

SECONDARY COVERAGE: Cover 1. The strong safety, Stud, and Whip drop into coverage and the free safety plays center field.

STUD: Plays 8 technique versus run. Drops **Abel** versus pass.

BUCK: Slants to the near shoulder of the offensive tackle and controls the C gap. Contains the quarterback versus pass.

STRONG SAFETY: Plays base technique versus run. Drops **Baker** versus pass.

STRONG TACKLE: Slants across the offensive guard's face into the strongside A gap.

NOSE: Loops across the face of the weakside offensive tackle. Secures the C gap and contains the quarterback.

WEAK TACKLE: Slants across the face of the offensive guard into the weakside A gap.

WEAK END: Slants across the offensive tackle's face into the B gap.

WHIP: Plays base technique versus run. Drops **Charlie** versus pass.

FREE SAFETY: Lines up as though he's playing cover 3. Provides alley support versus run. Plays center field versus pass.

STRONG CORNER: Covers receiver #1 (inside/outside technique dependent upon field position and the distance of the flanker's split).

WEAK CORNER: Covers receiver #1 (inside/outside technique dependent upon field position and the distance of the split end's split).

STUNT #43

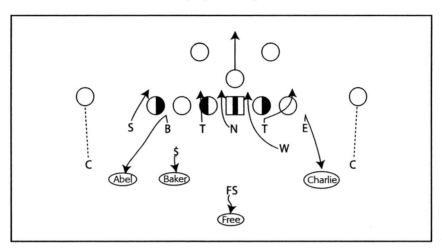

STUNT DESCRIPTION: This *fire zone blitz* sends both Stud and Whip.

SECONDARY COVERAGE: Cover 1. The weak end, Buck and the strong safety drop into coverage and the free safety plays center field.

STUD: Rushes from the edge. Contains the quarterback and strongside run. Chases weakside run.

BUCK: Plays 7 technique versus run. Drops **Abel** versus pass.

STRONG SAFETY: Plays base technique versus run. Drops **Baker** versus pass.

STRONG TACKLE: Plays 3 technique.

NOSE: Slants into the strongside A gap.

WEAK TACKLE: Plays 3 technique versus run. Contain rushes versus pass.

WEAK END: Plays 7 technique versus run. Drops **Charlie** versus pass.

WHIP: Blitzes through the weakside A gap.

FREE SAFETY: Lines up as though he's playing cover 3. Provides alley support versus run. Plays center field versus pass.

STRONG CORNER: Covers receiver #1 (inside/outside technique dependent upon field position and the distance of the flanker's split).

WEAK CORNER: Covers receiver #1 (inside/outside technique dependent upon field position and the distance of the split end's split).

STUNT #44

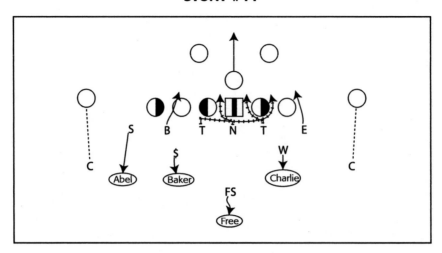

STUNT DESCRIPTION: This *fire zone blitz* sends Buck and provides the defense with a delayed weakside line twist versus pass.

SECONDARY COVERAGE: Cover 1. The strong safety, Stud, and Whip drop into coverage and the free safety plays center field.

STUD: Plays 8 technique versus run. Drops **Abel** versus pass.

BUCK: Slants to the near shoulder of the offensive tackle and controls the C gap. Contains the quarterback versus pass.

STRONG SAFETY: Plays base technique versus run. Drops **Baker** versus pass.

STRONG TACKLE: Plays 3 technique versus run. Loops into the weakside B gap versus pass.

NOSE: Plays 0 technique versus run. Slants through the strongside A gap versus pass.

WEAK TACKLE: Plays 3 technique versus run. Slants through the weakside A gap versus pass.

WEAK END: Plays 7 technique versus run. Contains the quarterback versus pass.

WHIP: Plays base technique versus run. Drops **Charlie** versus pass.

FREE SAFETY: Lines up as though he's playing cover 3. Provides alley support versus run. Plays center field versus pass.

STRONG CORNER: Covers receiver #1 (inside/outside technique dependent upon field position and the distance of the flanker's split).

WEAK CORNER: Covers receiver #1 (inside/outside technique dependent upon field position and the distance of the split end's split).

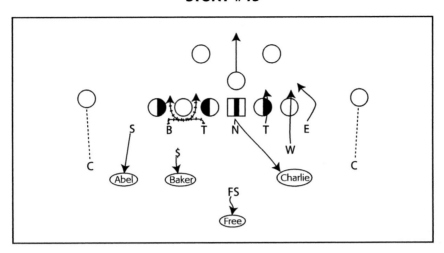

STUNT DESCRIPTION: This *fire zone blitz* sends Whip and provides the defense with a strongside line twist.

SECONDARY COVERAGE: Cover 1. The strong safety, Stud, and nose drop into coverage and the free safety plays center field.

STUD: Plays 8 technique versus run. Drops **Abel** versus pass.

BUCK: Plays 7 technique versus run. Loops behind the defensive tackle into the B gap versus pass.

STRONG SAFETY: Plays base technique versus run. Drops **Baker** versus pass.

STRONG TACKLE: Plays 3 technique versus run. Contains rush versus pass.

NOSE: Plays 0 technique versus run. Drops **Charlie** versus pass.

WEAK TACKLE: Plays 3 technique.

WEAK END: Slants outside. Contains the quarterback and weakside run. Chases strongside run.

WHIP: Blitzes through the outside shoulder of the offensive tackle and secures the C gap.

FREE SAFETY: Lines up as though he's playing cover 3. Provides alley support versus run. Plays center field versus pass.

STRONG CORNER: Covers receiver #1 (inside/outside technique dependent upon field position and the distance of the flanker's split).

WEAK CORNER: Covers receiver #1 (inside/outside technique dependent upon field position and the distance of the split end's split).

STUNT #46

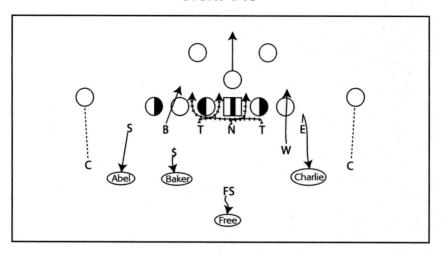

STUNT DESCRIPTION: This *fire zone blitz* sends Buck and Whip and provides the defense with a strongside line twist.

SECONDARY COVERAGE: Cover 1. The strong safety, Stud, and the weak end drop into coverage and the free safety plays center field.

STUD: Plays 8 technique versus run. Drops **Abel** versus pass.

BUCK: Attacks the near shoulder of the offensive tackle. Secures the C gap and contains the quarterback.

STRONG SAFETY: Plays base technique versus run. Drops **Baker** versus pass.

STRONG TACKLE: Plays 3 technique versus run. Slants into the A gap versus pass.

NOSE: Plays 0 technique versus run. Slants into the weakside A gap versus pass.

WEAK TACKLE: Plays 3 technique versus run. Loops into the strongside B gap versus pass.

WEAK END: Plays 7 technique versus run. Drops **Charlie** versus pass.

WHIP: Blitzes through the outside shoulder of the offensive tackle and secures the C gap.

FREE SAFETY: Lines up as though he's playing cover 3. Provides alley support versus run. Plays center field versus pass.

STRONG CORNER: Covers receiver #1 (inside/outside technique dependent upon field position and the distance of the flanker's split).

WEAK CORNER: Covers receiver #1 (inside/outside technique dependent upon field position and the distance of the split end's split).

STUNT #47

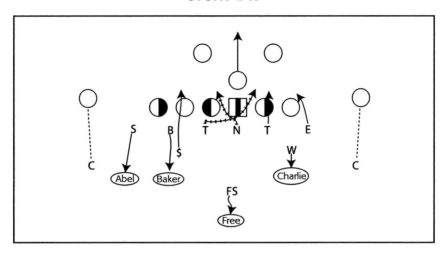

STUNT DESCRIPTION: This *fire zone blitz* sends the strong safety and provides the defense with a delayed line twist.

SECONDARY COVERAGE: Cover 1. Stud, Buck, and Whip drop into coverage and the free safety plays center field.

STUD: Plays 8 technique versus run. Drops **Abel** versus pass.

BUCK: Plays 7 technique versus run. Drops **Baker** versus pass.

STRONG SAFETY: Blitzes through the outside shoulder of the offensive tackle. Secures the C gap and contains the quarterback.

STRONG TACKLE: Plays 3 technique versus run. Loops behind the nose into the weakside A gap versus pass.

NOSE: Plays 0 technique versus run. Slants into the strongside A gap versus pass.

WEAK TACKLE: Plays 3 technique.

WEAK END: Plays 7 technique versus run. Contains the quarterback versus pass.

WHIP: Plays base technique versus run. Drops **Charlie** versus pass.

FREE SAFETY: Lines up as though he's playing cover 3. Provides alley support versus run. Plays center field versus pass.

STRONG CORNER: Covers receiver #1 (inside/outside technique dependent upon field position and the distance of the flanker's split).

WEAK CORNER: Covers receiver #1 (inside/outside technique dependent upon field position and the distance of the split end's split).

STUNT #48

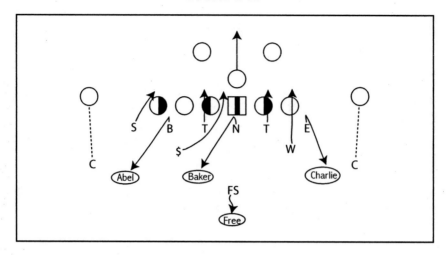

STUNT DESCRIPTION: This *fire zone blitz* sends the strong safety, Stud, and Whip.

SECONDARY COVERAGE: Cover 1. Buck, nose and the weak end drop into coverage and the free safety plays center field.

STUD: Rushes from the edge. Contains the quarterback and strongside run. Chases weakside run.

BUCK: Plays 7 technique versus run. Drops **Abel** versus pass.

STRONG SAFETY: Blitzes through the strongside A gap.

STRONG TACKLE: Plays 3 technique.

NOSE: Plays 0 technique versus run. Drops **Baker** versus pass.

WEAK TACKLE: Plays 3 technique.

WEAK END: Plays 7 technique versus run. Drops **Charlie** versus pass.

WHIP: Blitzes through the outside shoulder of the offensive tackle. Secures the C gap versus run and contains the quarterback versus pass.

FREE SAFETY: Lines up as though he's playing cover 3. Provides alley support versus run. Plays center field versus pass.

STRONG CORNER: Covers receiver #1 (inside/outside technique dependent upon field position and the distance of the flanker's split).

WEAK CORNER: Covers receiver #1 (inside/outside technique dependent upon field position and the distance of the split end's split).

STUNT #49

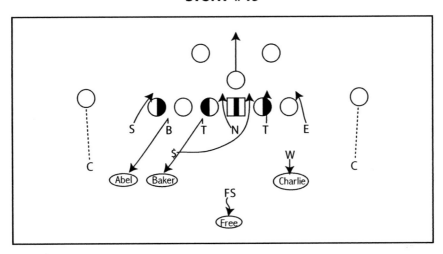

STUNT DESCRIPTION: This *fire zone blitz* sends the strong safety and Stud.

SECONDARY COVERAGE: Cover 1. Buck, the strong tackle, and Whip drop into coverage and the free safety plays center field.

STUD: Rushes from the edge. Contains the quarterback and strongside run. Chases weakside run.

BUCK: Plays 7 technique versus run. Drops **Abel** versus pass.

STRONG SAFETY: Blitzes through the weakside A gap.

STRONG TACKLE: Plays 3 technique versus run. Drops **Baker** versus pass.

NOSE: Slants into the strongside A gap.

WEAK TACKLE: Plays 3 technique.

WEAK END: Plays 7 technique versus run. Contains the quarterback versus pass.

WHIP: Plays base technique versus run. Drops **Charlie** versus pass.

FREE SAFETY: Lines up as though he's playing cover 3. Provides alley support versus run. Plays center field versus pass.

STRONG CORNER: Covers receiver #1 (inside/outside technique dependent upon field position and the distance of the flanker's split).

WEAK CORNER: Covers receiver #1 (inside/outside technique dependent upon field position and the distance of the split end's split).

STUNT #50

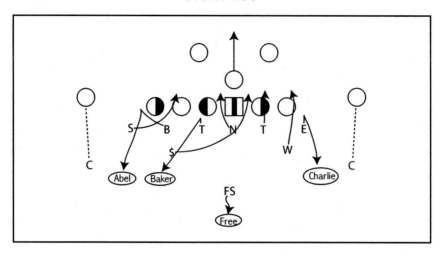

STUNT DESCRIPTION: This *fire zone blitz* sends the strong safety, Stud, and Whip.

SECONDARY COVERAGE: Cover 1. Buck, the strong tackle, and weak end drop into coverage and the free safety plays center field.

STUD: Blitzes through the near shoulder of the offensive tackle. Secures the C gap and contains the quarterback.

BUCK: Slants across the face of the tight end into the D gap. Contains strongside run, chases weakside run, and drops **Abel** versus pass.

STRONG SAFETY: Blitzes through the weakside A gap.

STRONG TACKLE: Plays 3 technique versus run. Drops **Baker** versus pass.

NOSE: Slants into the strongside A gap.

WEAK TACKLE: Plays 3 technique.

WEAK END: Plays 7 technique versus run. Drops **Charlie** versus pass.

WHIP: Blitzes through the outside shoulder of the offensive tackle. Secures the C gap and contains the quarterback.

FREE SAFETY: Lines up as though he's playing cover 3. Provides alley support versus run. Plays center field versus pass.

STRONG CORNER: Covers receiver #1 (inside/outside technique dependent upon field position and the distance of the flanker's split).

WEAK CORNER: Covers receiver #1 (inside/outside technique dependent upon field position and the distance of the split end's split).

STUNT #51

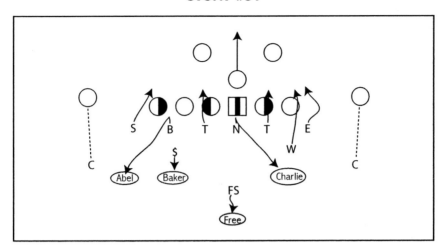

STUNT DESCRIPTION: This *fire zone blitz* sends Whip and Stud.

SECONDARY COVERAGE: Cover 1. Buck, the nose, and the strong safety drop into coverage and the free safety plays center field.

STUD: Rushes from the edge. Contains the quarterback and strongside run. Chases weakside run.

BUCK: Plays 7 technique versus run. Drops **Abel** versus pass.

STRONG SAFETY: Plays base technique versus run. Drops **Baker** versus pass.

STRONG TACKLE: Plays 3 technique.

NOSE: Plays 0 technique versus run. Drops **Charlie** versus pass.

WEAK TACKLE: Plays 3 technique.

WEAK END: Slants outside. Contains the quarterback and weakside run. Chases strongside run.

WHIP: Blitzes through the outside shoulder of the offensive tackle and secures the C gap.

FREE SAFETY: Lines up as though he's playing cover 3. Provides alley support versus run. Plays center field versus pass.

STRONG CORNER: Covers receiver #1 (inside/outside technique dependent upon field position and the distance of the flanker's split).

WEAK CORNER: Covers receiver #1 (inside/outside technique dependent upon field position and the distance of the split end's split).

STUNT #52

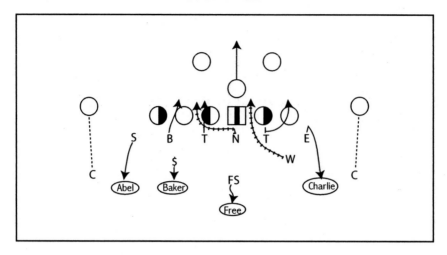

STUNT DESCRIPTION: This *fire zone blitz* provides the defense with a delayed blitz by Whip and a delayed strongside twin stunt.

SECONDARY COVERAGE: Cover 1. The strong safety, Stud, and the weak end drop into coverage and the free safety plays center field.

STUD: Plays 8 technique versus run. Drops **Abel** versus pass.

BUCK: Attacks the near shoulder of the offensive tackle. Secures the C gap and contains the quarterback.

STRONG SAFETY: Plays base technique versus run. Drops **Baker** versus pass.

STRONG TACKLE: Plays 3 technique.

NOSE: Plays 0 technique versus run. Loops into the strongside B gap (twin stunt) versus pass.

WEAK TACKLE: Plays 3 technique versus run. Contain rushes versus pass.

WEAK END: Plays 7 technique versus run. Drops **Charlie** versus pass.

WHIP: Plays base technique versus run. Delay blitzes through the weakside A gap versus pass.

FREE SAFETY: Lines up as though he's playing cover 3. Provides alley support versus run. Plays center field versus pass.

STRONG CORNER: Covers receiver #1 (inside/outside technique dependent upon field position and the distance of the flanker's split).

WEAK CORNER: Covers receiver #1 (inside/outside technique dependent upon field position and the distance of the split end's split).

STUNT #53

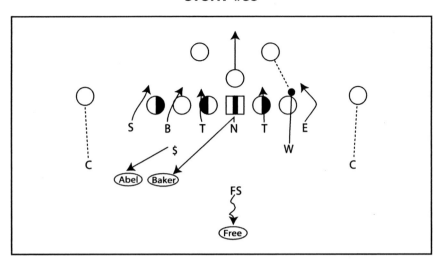

STUNT DESCRIPTION: This *hybrid fire zone blitz* sends Stud and Buck.

SECONDARY COVERAGE: Cover 1. The strong safety and nose drop into coverage and Whip spies the near back. The free safety plays center field.

STUD: Rushes from the edge. Contains the quarterback and strongside run. Chases weakside run.

BUCK: Attacks the near shoulder of the offensive tackle and controls the C gap.

STRONG SAFETY: Plays base technique versus run. Drops **Abel** versus pass.

STRONG TACKLE: Plays 3 technique.

NOSE: Plays 0 technique versus run. Drops **Baker** versus pass.

WEAK TACKLE: Plays 3 technique.

WEAK END: Slants outside and secures the D gap versus run. Contains the quarterback versus pass.

WHIP: Attacks the outside shoulder of the offensive tackle. Controls the C gap versus run and spies the near back versus pass.

FREE SAFETY: Lines up as though he's playing cover 3. Provides alley support versus run. Plays center field versus pass.

STRONG CORNER: Covers receiver #1 (inside/outside technique dependent upon field position and the distance of the flanker's split).

WEAK CORNER: Covers receiver #1 (inside/outside technique dependent upon field position and the distance of the split end's split).

STUNT #54

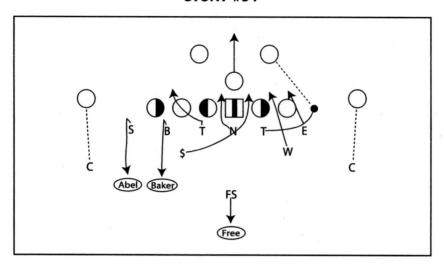

STUNT DESCRIPTION: This *hybrid fire zone blitz* sends the strong safety and Whip.

SECONDARY COVERAGE: Cover 1. Stud and Buck drops into coverage and the weak tackle spies the near back. The free safety plays center field.

STUD: Plays 8 technique versus run. Drops **Abel** versus pass.

BUCK: Plays 7 technique versus run. Drops **Baker** versus pass.

STRONG SAFETY: Blitzes through the weakside A gap.

STRONG TACKLE: Plays 3 technique versus run. Contain rushes versus pass.

NOSE: Slants into the strongside A gap.

WEAK TACKLE: Loops outside and secures the D gap versus run. Spies the near back versus pass.

WEAK END: Attacks the near shoulder of the offensive tackle. Controls the C gap versus run and contains the quarterback versus pass.

WHIP: Blitzes through the weakside B gap.

FREE SAFETY: Lines up as though he's playing cover 3. Provides alley support versus run. Plays center field versus pass.

STRONG CORNER: Covers receiver #1 (inside/outside technique dependent upon field position and the distance of the flanker's split).

WEAK CORNER: Covers receiver #1 (inside/outside technique dependent upon field position and the distance of the split end's split).

STUNT #55

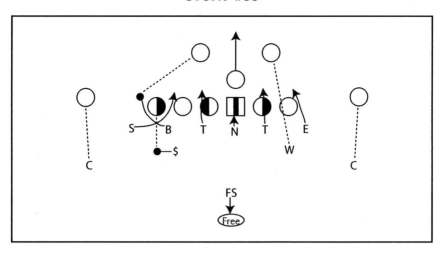

STUNT DESCRIPTION: This *dog* sends Stud.

SECONDARY COVERAGE: Cover 1. The strong safety covers the tight end. Buck and Whip cover the near backs, and the free safety plays center field.

STUD: Loops behind Buck and attacks the near shoulder of the offensive tackle. Secures the C gap and contains the quarterback.

BUCK: Slants outside. Secures the D gap versus run and spies the near back versus pass.

STRONG SAFETY: Covers the tight end.

STRONG TACKLE: Plays 3 technique.

NOSE: Plays 0 technique.

WEAK TACKLE: Plays 3 technique.

WEAK END: Plays 7 technique versus run. Contains the quarterback versus pass.

WHIP: Plays base technique versus run. Covers the near back versus pass.

FREE SAFETY: Lines up as though he's playing cover 3. Provides alley support versus run. Plays center field versus pass.

STRONG CORNER: Covers receiver #1 (inside/outside technique dependent upon field position and the distance of the flanker's split).

WEAK CORNER: Covers receiver #1 (inside/outside technique dependent upon field position and the distance of the split end's split).

STUNT #56

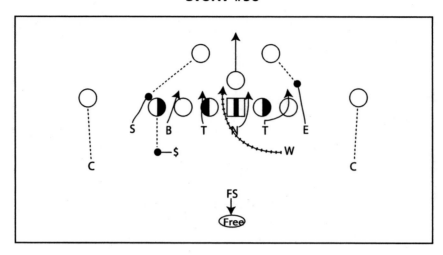

STUNT DESCRIPTION: This *dog* sends Whip.

SECONDARY COVERAGE: Cover 1. The strong safety covers the tight end. Stud and the weak end cover the near backs, and the free safety plays center field.

STUD: Gives the impression that he's rushing from the edge. Contains strongside run and chases weakside run. Spies the near back versus pass.

BUCK: Attacks the near shoulder of the offensive tackle. Controls the C gap versus run and contains the quarterback versus pass.

STRONG SAFETY: Covers the tight end.

STRONG TACKLE: Plays 3 technique.

NOSE: Slants into the weakside A gap.

WEAK TACKLE: Plays 3 technique versus run. Contain rushes versus pass.

WEAK END: Plays 7 technique versus run. Spies the near back versus pass.

WHIP: Plays base technique versus run. Delay rushes through strongside A gap versus pass.

FREE SAFETY: Lines up as though he's playing cover 3. Provides alley support versus run. Plays center field versus pass.

STRONG CORNER: Covers receiver #1 (inside/outside technique dependent upon field position and the distance of the flanker's split).

WEAK CORNER: Covers receiver #1 (inside/outside technique dependent upon field position and the distance of the split end's split).

STUNT #57

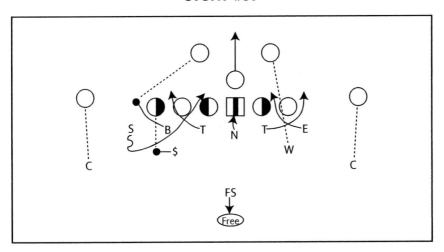

STUNT DESCRIPTION: This *dog* sends Stud and provides the defense with a weakside line twist.

SECONDARY COVERAGE: Cover 1. The strong safety covers the tight end. Buck and Whip cover the near backs, and the free safety plays center field.

STUD: Sinks back during cadence and gives the impression that he's covering the tight end. Blitzes through the strongside B gap at the snap.

BUCK: Slants outside. Secures the D gap versus run and spies the near back versus pass.

STRONG SAFETY: Covers the tight end.

STRONG TACKLE: Slants to the far shoulder of the offensive tackle. Controls the C gap versus run and contains the quarterback versus pass.

NOSE: Plays 0 technique.

WEAK TACKLE: Loops behind the weak end. Secures the C gap versus run and contains the quarterback versus pass.

WEAK END: Slants into the B gap.

WHIP: Plays base technique versus run. Covers the near back versus pass.

FREE SAFETY: Lines up as though he's playing cover 3. Provides alley support versus run. Plays center field versus pass.

STRONG CORNER: Covers receiver #1 (inside/outside technique dependent upon field position and the distance of the flanker's split).

WEAK CORNER: Covers receiver #1 (inside/outside technique dependent upon field position and the distance of the split end's split).

STUNT #58

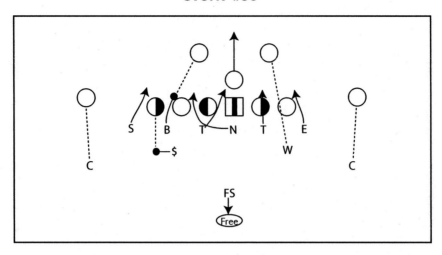

STUNT DESCRIPTION: This *dog* sends Stud and provides the defense with a strongside line twist.

SECONDARY COVERAGE: Cover 1. The strong safety covers the tight end. Buck and Whip cover the near backs, and the free safety plays center field.

STUD: Rushes from the edge. Contains the quarterback and strongside run. Chases weakside run.

BUCK: Attacks the near shoulder of the offensive tackle. Controls the C gap versus run and spies the near back versus pass.

STRONG SAFETY: Covers the tight end.

STRONG TACKLE: Slants into the A gap.

NOSE: Loops behind the strong tackle and attacks the far shoulder of the offensive guard. Secures the B gap.

WEAK TACKLE: Plays 3 technique.

WEAK END: Plays 7 technique versus run. Contains the quarterback versus pass.

WHIP: Plays base technique versus run. Covers the near back versus pass.

FREE SAFETY: Lines up as though he's playing cover 3. Provides alley support versus run. Plays center field versus pass.

STRONG CORNER: Covers receiver #1 (inside/outside technique dependent upon field position and the distance of the flanker's split).

WEAK CORNER: Covers receiver #1 (inside/outside technique dependent upon field position and the distance of the split end's split).

STUNT #59

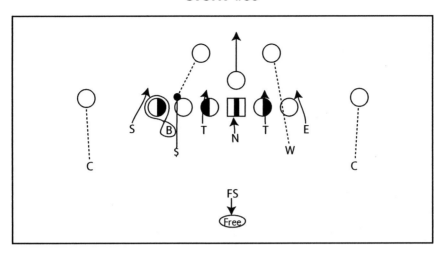

STUNT DESCRIPTION: This *dog* sends Stud.

SECONDARY COVERAGE: Cover 1. Buck covers the tight end. The strong safety and Whip cover the near backs, and the free safety plays center field.

STUD: Rushes from the edge. Contains the quarterback and strongside run. Chases weakside run.

BUCK: Covers the tight end.

STRONG SAFETY: Sells blitz by attacking the outside shoulder of the offensive tackle at the snap. Secures the C gap versus run and spies the near back versus pass.

STRONG TACKLE: Plays 3 technique.

NOSE: Plays 0 technique.

WEAK TACKLE: Plays 3 technique.

WEAK END: Plays 7 technique versus run. Contains the quarterback versus pass.

WHIP: Plays base technique versus run. Covers the near back versus pass.

FREE SAFETY: Lines up as though he's playing cover 3. Provides alley support versus run. Plays center field versus pass.

STRONG CORNER: Covers receiver #1 (inside/outside technique dependent upon field position and the distance of the flanker's split).

WEAK CORNER: Covers receiver #1 (inside/outside technique dependent upon field position and the distance of the split end's split).

STUNT #60

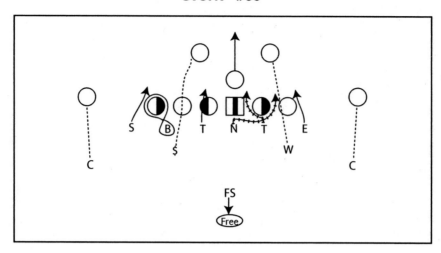

STUNT DESCRIPTION: This *dog* sends Stud and provides the defense with a weakside delayed line twist versus pass.

SECONDARY COVERAGE: Cover 1. Buck covers the tight end. The strong safety and Whip cover the near backs, and the free safety plays center field.

STUD: Rushes from the edge. Contains the quarterback and strongside run. Chases weakside run.

BUCK: Covers the tight end.

STRONG SAFETY: Plays base technique versus run. Covers the near back versus pass.

STRONG TACKLE: Plays 3 technique.

NOSE: Plays 0 technique versus run. Loops behind the weak tackle into the weakside B gap versus pass.

WEAK TACKLE: Plays 3 technique versus run. Quickly penetrates the A gap versus pass.

WEAK END: Plays 7 technique versus run. Contains the quarterback versus pass.

WHIP: Plays base technique versus run. Covers the near back versus pass.

FREE SAFETY: Lines up as though he's playing cover 3. Provides alley support versus run. Plays center field versus pass.

STRONG CORNER: Covers receiver #1 (inside/outside technique dependent upon field position and the distance of the flanker's split).

WEAK CORNER: Covers receiver #1 (inside/outside technique dependent upon field position and the distance of the split end's split).

STUNT #61

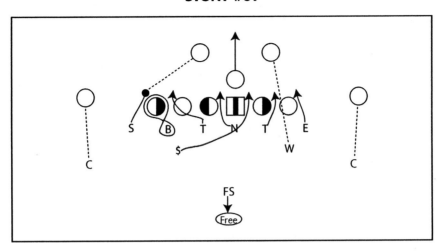

STUNT DESCRIPTION: This *dog* sends the strong safety.

SECONDARY COVERAGE: Cover 1. Buck covers the tight end. Stud and Whip cover the near backs, and the free safety plays center field.

STUD: Gives the impression that he's rushing from the edge. Contains strongside run and chases weakside run. Spies the near back versus pass.

BUCK: Covers the tight end.

STRONG SAFETY: Blitzes through the weakside A gap.

STRONG TACKLE: Plays 3 technique versus run. Contain rushes versus pass.

NOSE: Slants into the strongside A gap.

WEAK TACKLE: Plays 3 technique.

WEAK END: Plays 7 technique versus run. Contains the quarterback versus pass.

WHIP: Plays base technique versus run. Covers the near back versus pass.

FREE SAFETY: Lines up as though he's playing cover 3. Provides alley support versus run. Plays center field versus pass.

STRONG CORNER: Covers receiver #1 (inside/outside technique dependent upon field position and the distance of the flanker's split).

WEAK CORNER: Covers receiver #1 (inside/outside technique dependent upon field position and the distance of the split end's split).

STUNT #62

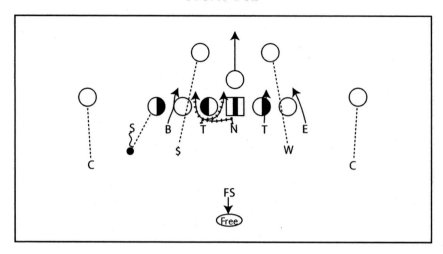

STUNT DESCRIPTION: This dog sends Buck and provides the defense with a strongside delayed line twist versus pass.

SECONDARY COVERAGE: Cover 1. Stud covers the tight end. The strong safety and Whip cover the near backs, and the free safety plays center field.

STUD: Sinks back during cadence. Plays 8 technique versus run. Covers the tight end versus pass.

BUCK: Attacks the near shoulder of the offensive tackle. Controls the C gap versus run and contains the quarterback versus pass.

STRONG SAFETY: Plays base technique versus run. Covers the near back versus pass.

STRONG TACKLE: Plays 3 technique versus run. Quickly penetrates the A gap versus pass.

NOSE: Plays 0 technique versus run. Loops behind the strong tackle into the strongside B gap versus pass.

WEAK TACKLE: Plays 3 technique.

WEAK END: Plays 7 technique versus run. Contains the quarterback versus pass.

WHIP: Plays base technique versus run. Covers the near back versus pass.

FREE SAFETY: Lines up as though he's playing cover 3. Provides alley support versus run. Plays center field versus pass.

STRONG CORNER: Covers receiver #1 (inside/outside technique dependent upon field position and the distance of the flanker's split).

WEAK CORNER: Covers receiver #1 (inside/outside technique dependent upon field position and the distance of the split end's split).

STUNT #63

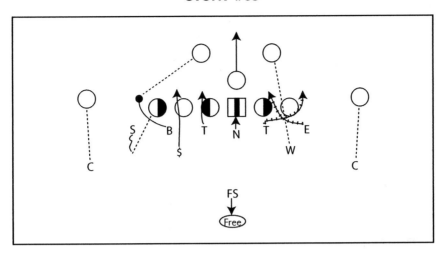

STUNT DESCRIPTION: This *dog* sends the strong safety and provides the defense with a weakside delayed line twist versus pass.

SECONDARY COVERAGE: Cover 1. Stud covers the tight end. The strong safety and Whip cover the near backs, and the free safety plays center field.

STUD: Sinks back during cadence. Plays 8 technique versus run. Covers the tight end versus pass.

BUCK: Slants outside and secures the D gap versus run. Spies the near back versus pass.

STRONG SAFETY: Blitzes through the outside shoulder of the offensive tackle. Controls C gap versus run and contains the quarterback versus pass.

STRONG TACKLE: Plays 3 technique.

NOSE: Plays 0 technique.

WEAK TACKLE: Plays 3 technique versus run. Loops behind the weak end and contains the quarterback versus pass.

WEAK END: Plays 7 technique versus run. Quickly penetrates the B gap versus pass.

WHIP: Plays base technique versus run. Covers the near back versus pass.

FREE SAFETY: Lines up as though he's playing cover 3. Provides alley support versus run. Plays center field versus pass.

STRONG CORNER: Covers receiver #1 (inside/outside technique dependent upon field position and the distance of the flanker's split).

WEAK CORNER: Covers receiver #1 (inside/outside technique dependent upon field position and the distance of the split end's split).

STUNT #64

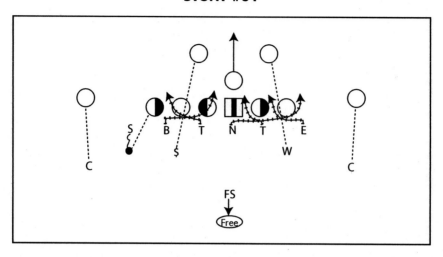

STUNT DESCRIPTION: This *dog* sends Buck and provides the defense with both a strong and weakside delayed line twist versus pass.

SECONDARY COVERAGE: Cover 1. Stud covers the tight end. The strong safety and Whip cover the near backs, and the free safety plays center field.

STUD: Sinks back during cadence. Plays 8 technique versus run. Covers the tight end versus pass.

BUCK: Plays 7 technique versus run. Loops behind the strong tackle into the B gap versus pass.

STRONG SAFETY: Plays base technique versus run. Covers the near back versus pass.

STRONG TACKLE: Plays 3 technique versus run. Contains rush versus pass.

NOSE: Plays 0 technique versus run. Loops to the outside shoulder of the offensive tackle and contains the quarterback versus pass.

WEAK TACKLE: Plays 3 technique versus run. Quickly penetrates the A gap versus pass.

WEAK END: Plays 7 technique versus run. Quickly penetrates the B gap versus pass.

WHIP: Plays base technique versus run. Covers the near back versus pass.

FREE SAFETY: Lines up as though he's playing cover 3. Provides alley support versus run. Plays center field versus pass.

STRONG CORNER: Covers receiver #1 (inside/outside technique dependent upon field position and the distance of the flanker's split).

WEAK CORNER: Covers receiver #1 (inside/outside technique dependent upon field position and the distance of the split end's split).

STUNT #65

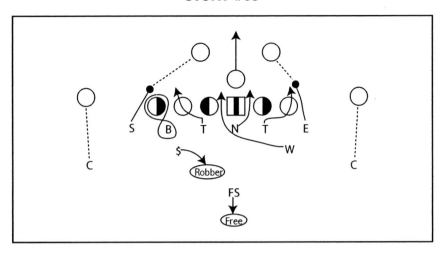

STUNT DESCRIPTION: This stunt gives the offense the *illusion* of a six-man pass rush and provides the defense with robber coverage.

SECONDARY COVERAGE: Cover 1 robber. The strong safety is the robber. Buck covers the tight end, and the weak end and Stud spy the near backs. The free safety plays center field.

STUD: Gives the impression that he's rushing from the edge. Contains strongside run and chases weakside run. Spies the near back versus pass.

BUCK: Covers the tight end.

STRONG SAFETY: Plays base technique versus run. Drops robber versus pass.

STRONG TACKLE: Plays 3 technique versus run. Contain rushes versus pass.

NOSE: Slants into the weakside A gap.

WEAK TACKLE: Plays 3 technique versus run. Contain rushes versus pass.

WEAK END: Plays 7 technique versus run. Spies the near back versus pass.

WHIP: Blitzes through the strongside A gap.

FREE SAFETY: Lines up as though he's playing cover 3. Provides alley support versus run. Plays center field versus pass.

STRONG CORNER: Covers receiver #1 (inside/outside technique dependent upon field position and the distance of the flanker's split).

WEAK CORNER: Covers receiver #1 (inside/outside technique dependent upon field position and the distance of the split end's split).

STUNT #66

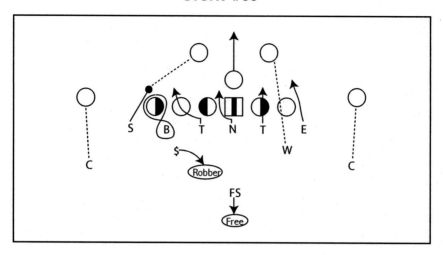

STUNT DESCRIPTION: This stunt gives the offense the *illusion* of a five-man pass rush and provides the defense with robber coverage.

SECONDARY COVERAGE: Cover 1 robber. The strong safety is the robber. Buck covers the tight end. Whip and Stud cover the near backs, and the free safety plays center field.

STUD: Gives the impression that he's rushing from the edge. Contains strongside run and chases weakside run. Spies the near back versus pass.

BUCK: Covers the tight end.

STRONG SAFETY: Plays base technique versus run. Drops robber versus pass.

STRONG TACKLE: Plays 3 technique versus run. Contain rushes versus pass.

NOSE: Plays 0 technique versus run. Rushes through the strongside A gap versus pass.

WEAK TACKLE: Plays 3 technique.

WEAK END: Plays 7 technique versus run. Contains the quarterback versus pass.

WHIP: Plays base technique versus run. Covers the near back versus pass.

FREE SAFETY: Lines up as though he's playing cover 3. Provides alley support versus run. Plays center field versus pass.

STRONG CORNER: Covers receiver #1 (inside/outside technique dependent upon field position and the distance of the flanker's split).

WEAK CORNER: Covers receiver #1 (inside/outside technique dependent upon field position and the distance of the split end's split).

STUNT #67

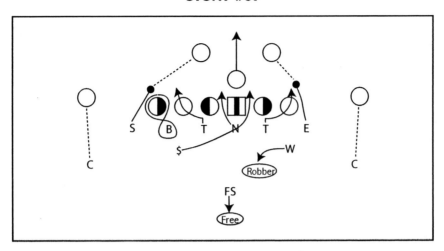

STUNT DESCRIPTION: This stunt gives the offense the *illusion* of a six-man pass rush and provides the defense with robber coverage.

SECONDARY COVERAGE: Cover 1 robber. Whip is the robber. Buck covers the tight end. The weak end and Stud cover the near backs, and the free safety plays center field.

STUD: Gives the impression that he's rushing from the edge. Contains strongside run and chases weakside run. Spies the near back versus pass.

BUCK: Covers the tight end.

STRONG SAFETY: Blitzes through the weakside A gap.

STRONG TACKLE: Plays 3 technique versus run. Contain rushes versus pass.

NOSE: Plays 0 technique versus run. Rushes through the strongside A gap versus pass.

WEAK TACKLE: Plays 3 technique versus run. Contain rushes versus pass.

WEAK END: Plays 7 technique versus run. Spies the near back versus pass.

WHIP: Plays base technique versus run. Drops robber versus pass.

FREE SAFETY: Lines up as though he's playing cover 3. Provides alley support versus run. Plays center field versus pass.

STRONG CORNER: Covers receiver #1 (inside/outside technique dependent upon field position and the distance of the flanker's split).

WEAK CORNER: Covers receiver #1 (inside/outside technique dependent upon field position and the distance of the split end's split).

STUNT #68

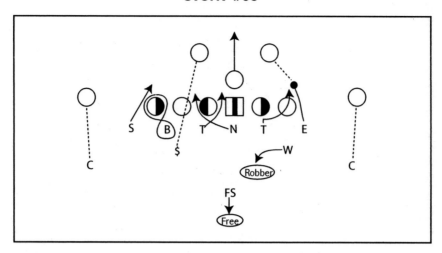

STUNT DESCRIPTION: This robber coverage stunt gives the offense the *illusion* of a five-man pass rush and a strongside line twist.

SECONDARY COVERAGE: Cover 1 robber. Whip is the robber. Buck covers the tight end. The weak end and strong safety cover the near backs, and the free safety plays center field.

STUD: Rushes from the edge. Contains the quarterback and strongside run. Chases weakside run.

BUCK: Covers the tight end.

STRONG SAFETY: Plays base technique versus run. Covers the near back versus pass.

STRONG TACKLE: Slants into the A gap.

NOSE: Loops behind the strong tackle to the far shoulder of the offensive guard and secures the strongside B gap.

WEAK TACKLE: Plays 3 technique versus run. Contain rushes versus pass.

WEAK END: Plays 7 technique versus run. Spies the near back versus pass.

WHIP: Plays base technique versus run. Drops robber versus pass.

FREE SAFETY: Lines up as though he's playing cover 3. Provides alley support to run. Plays center field versus pass.

STRONG CORNER: Covers receiver #1 (inside/outside technique dependent upon field position and the distance of the flanker's split).

WEAK CORNER: Covers receiver #1 (inside/outside technique dependent upon field position and the distance of the split end's split).

STUNT #69

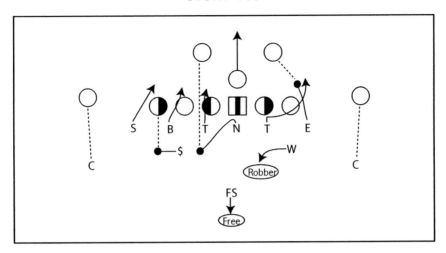

STUNT DESCRIPTION: This robber coverage stunt gives the offense the *illusion* of a six-man pass rush.

SECONDARY COVERAGE: Cover 1 robber. Whip is the robber. The strong safety covers the tight end. The weak end and nose cover the near backs, and the free safety plays center field.

STUD: Rushes from the edge. Contains the quarterback and strongside run. Chases weakside run.

BUCK: Attacks the near shoulder of the offensive tackle and controls the C gap.

STRONG SAFETY: Covers the tight end.

STRONG TACKLE: Plays 3 technique.

NOSE: Plays 0 technique versus run. Drops to a position that enables him to cover the strongside halfback versus pass.

WEAK TACKLE: Plays 3 technique versus run. Contain rushes versus pass.

WEAK END: Plays 7 technique versus run. Spies the near back versus pass.

WHIP: Plays base technique versus run. Drops robber versus pass.

FREE SAFETY: Lines up as though he's playing cover 3. Provides alley support versus run. Plays center field versus pass.

STRONG CORNER: Covers receiver #1 (inside/outside technique dependent upon field position and the distance of the flanker's split).

WEAK CORNER: Covers receiver #1 (inside/outside technique dependent upon field position and the distance of the split end's split).

CHAPTER 5

Cover 3 Stunts

The following pattern-read guidelines will assist defenders who drop into one of the cover 3 zones.

Strong Hook-Curl Drop

A defensive back should:

- Drop into the strong hook zone to a depth of 12-15 yards.
- Key #2 (the tight end).
- Stay in the hook zone and collision #2 if he runs a vertical route.
- Sprint to the curl and look for #1 (the flanker) to run a curl or a post if #2 releases into the flats.
- Try to collision #2 if he runs inside and across the defender's face, and then look for another receiver to run a crossing route into the defender's zone.

Weak Hook-Curl Drop

A defensive back should:

- Open up and drop into the weak hook zone to a depth of 12-15 yards. Key #2 (the weakside halfback).
- Stay in the hook zone and collision #2 if he runs a vertical route.

- Sprint to the curl and look for #1 (the split end) to run a curl or post if #2 releases into the flats.
- Try to collision #2 if he runs inside and across the defender's face, and then look for another receiver to run a crossing route into the defender's zone.

Strong Curl-Out Drop

A defensive back should:

- Open up and drop to a depth of 10-12 yards.
- Find an aiming point three yards inside of where #1 (the flanker) is lined up.
- Key #1.
- Try to get into the throwing lane and get a piece of the ball if #1 runs an out.
- Stay inside of #1's pattern if he runs a curl or a post, and check #2 (the tight end).
- Release from #1's curl or post if #2 crosses the defender's face while running an out.
- Sink and check #2 and #3 if #1 runs a vertical route.

Weak Curl-Out Drop

A defensive back should:

- Open up and drop to a depth of 10-12 yards.
- Find an aiming point three yards inside of where #1 (the split end) is lined up.
- Key #1.
- Try to get into the throwing lane and get a piece of the ball if #1 runs an out.
- Stay inside of #1's pattern if he runs a curl or a post and check #2 (the weakside halfback).
- Release from #1's curl or post if #2 crosses the defender's face while running an out.
- Sink and check #2 if #1 runs a vertical route.

Deep Outside Third Drop

A defensive back should:

- See both #1 and #2 as he backpedals.
- Stay as deep as the deepest receiver in his zone.
- Look for #2 to threaten deep if #1 runs a short or intermediate route.

- Control the speed of his backpedal so that he can break on the ball if #2 also runs a short or intermediate route.

- Maintain a cushion of 3-4 yards if #1 runs a vertical route.

- Stay on #1's outside hip and maintain a sufficient cushion if he runs a post.

Deep Middle Third Drop

A defensive back should:

- Drop midway between the two cornerbacks, stay as deep as the deepest receiver, and play center field.

- Key #2's release. If it is vertical, the defender must get into a position to cover it. If #2's route is short, the defender checks the split end and flanker for the post pattern.

STUNT #70

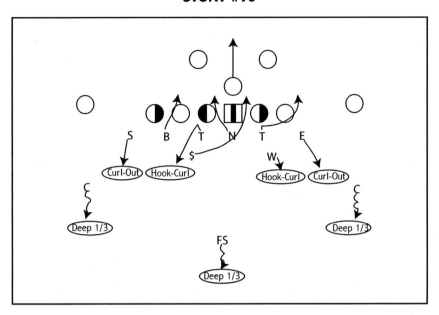

STUNT DESCRIPTION: This is an *old school zone blitz*.

SECONDARY COVERAGE: Cover 3. The strong safety and Buck blitz. Stud, Whip, the strong tackle, and the weak end drop into the under coverage.

STUD: Plays 8 technique versus run. Drops curl-out versus pass.

BUCK: Attacks the near shoulder of the offensive tackle and controls the C gap versus run. Contains the quarterback versus pass.

STRONG SAFETY: Blitzes through the weakside A gap.

STRONG TACKLE: Plays 3 technique versus run. Drops hook-curl versus pass.

NOSE: Slants into the strongside A gap.

WEAK TACKLE: Plays 3 technique versus run. Contain rushes versus pass.

WEAK END: Plays 7 technique versus run. Drops curl-out versus pass.

WHIP: Plays base technique versus run. Drops hook-curl versus pass.

FREE SAFETY: Covers the deep middle third.

STRONG CORNER: Covers the deep outside third.

WEAK CORNER: Covers the deep outside third.

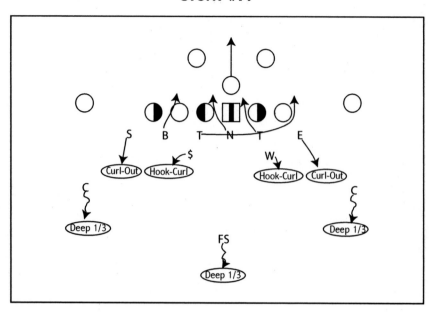

STUNT DESCRIPTION: This stunt sends Buck and provides the defense with a weakside line twist.

SECONDARY COVERAGE: Cover 3. Buck blitzes. Stud, Whip, the strong safety, and the weak end drop into the under coverage.

STUD: Plays 8 technique versus run. Drops curl-out versus pass.

BUCK: Attacks the near shoulder of the offensive tackle and controls the C gap versus run. Contains the quarterback versus pass.

STRONG SAFETY: Plays base technique versus run. Drops hook-curl versus pass.

STRONG TACKLE: Loops to the far shoulder of the offensive tackle. Secures the weakside C gap versus run and contains the quarterback versus pass.

NOSE: Slants into the strongside A gap.

WEAK TACKLE: Slants into the A gap.

WEAK END: Plays 7 technique versus run. Drops curl-out versus pass.

WHIP: Plays base technique versus run. Drops hook-curl versus pass.

FREE SAFETY: Covers the deep middle third.

STRONG CORNER: Cover the deep outside third.

WEAK CORNER: Cover the deep outside third.

STUNT #72

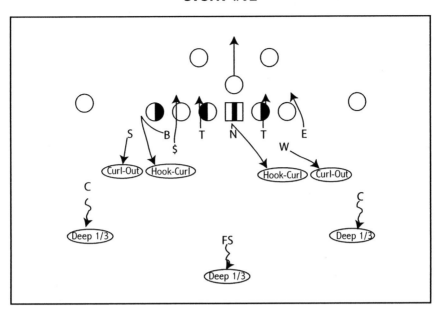

STUNT DESCRIPTION: This is an *old school zone blitz*.

SECONDARY COVERAGE: Cover 3. The strong safety blitzes. Stud, Buck, Whip, and the nose drop into the under coverage.

STUD: Plays 8 technique versus run. Drops curl-out versus pass.

BUCK: Slants outside and helps secure the D gap versus run. Drops hook-curl versus pass.

STRONG SAFETY: Blitzes through the outside shoulder of the offensive tackle. Controls the C gap versus run and contains the quarterback versus pass.

STRONG TACKLE: Plays 3 technique.

NOSE: Plays 0 technique versus run. Drops hook-curl versus pass.

WEAK TACKLE: Plays 3 technique.

WEAK END: Plays 7 technique versus run. Contains the quarterback versus pass.

WHIP: Plays base technique versus run. Drops curl-out versus pass.

FREE SAFETY: Covers the deep middle third.

STRONG CORNER: Covers the deep outside third.

WEAK CORNER: Covers the deep outside third.

STUNT #73

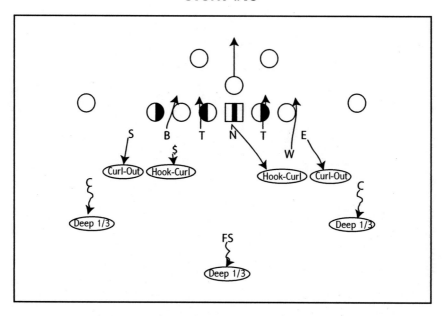

STUNT DESCRIPTION: This is an *old school zone blitz*.

SECONDARY COVERAGE: Cover 3. Buck and Whip blitz. Stud, nose, the strong safety, and the weak end drop into the under coverage.

STUD: Plays 8 technique versus run. Drops curl-out versus pass.

BUCK: Attacks the near shoulder of the offensive tackle. Secures the C gap versus run and contains the quarterback versus pass.

STRONG SAFETY: Plays base technique versus run. Drops hook-curl versus pass.

STRONG TACKLE: Plays 3 technique.

NOSE: Plays 0 technique versus run. Drops hook-curl versus pass.

WEAK TACKLE: Plays 3 technique.

WEAK END: Plays 7 technique versus run. Drops curl-out versus pass.

WHIP: Blitzes through the outside shoulder of the offensive tackle. Controls the C gap versus run and contains the quarterback versus pass.

FREE SAFETY: Covers the deep middle third.

STRONG CORNER: Covers the deep outside third.

WEAK CORNER: Covers the deep outside third.

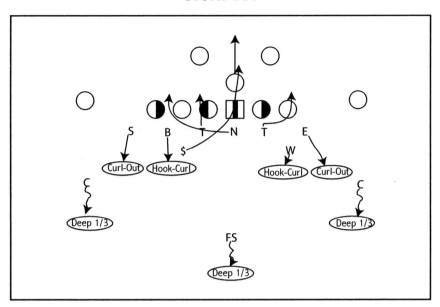

STUNT DESCRIPTION: This is an *old school zone blitz*.

SECONDARY COVERAGE: Cover 3. The strong safety blitzes. Stud, Buck, Whip, and the weak end drop into the under coverage.

STUD: Plays 8 technique versus run. Drops curl-out versus pass.

BUCK: Plays 7 technique versus run. Drops hook-curl versus pass.

STRONG SAFETY: Blitzes through the face of the center.

STRONG TACKLE: Plays 3 technique.

NOSE: Loops to the far shoulder of the offensive tackle and secures the C gap versus run. Contains the quarterback versus pass.

WEAK TACKLE: Plays 3 technique versus run. Contain rushes versus pass.

WEAK END: Plays 7 technique versus run. Drops curl-out versus pass.

WHIP: Plays base technique versus run. Drops hook-curl versus pass.

FREE SAFETY: Covers the deep middle third.

STRONG CORNER: Covers the deep outside third.

WEAK CORNER: Covers the deep outside third.

STUNT #75

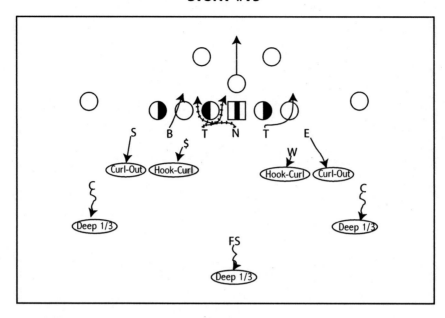

STUNT DESCRIPTION: This *old school zone blitz* sends Buck and provides the defense with a strongside delayed line twist versus pass.

SECONDARY COVERAGE: Cover 3. Buck blitzes. Stud, Whip, the strong safety, and the weak end drop into the under coverage.

STUD: Plays 8 technique versus run. Drops curl-out versus pass.

BUCK: Attacks the near shoulder of the offensive tackle. Secures the C gap versus run and contains the quarterback versus pass.

STRONG SAFETY: Plays base technique versus run. Drops hook-curl versus pass.

STRONG TACKLE: Plays 3 technique versus run. Quickly penetrates the A gap versus pass.

NOSE: Plays 0 technique versus run. Loops behind the left tackle into the strongside B gap versus pass.

WEAK TACKLE: Plays 3 technique versus run. Contain rushes versus pass.

WEAK END: Plays 7 technique versus run. Drops curl-out versus pass.

WHIP: Plays base technique versus run. Drops hook-curl versus pass.

FREE SAFETY: Covers the deep middle third.

STRONG CORNER: Covers the deep outside third.

WEAK CORNER: Covers the deep outside third.

CHAPTER 6

Secondary Blitzes and Fake Secondary Blitzes

STUNT #76

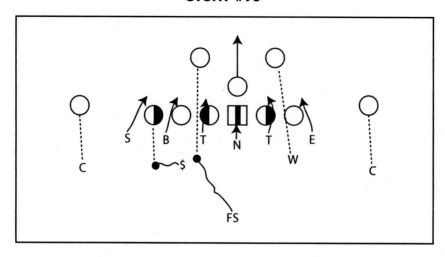

STUNT DESCRIPTION: This blitz features a *fake secondary blitz* by the free safety.

SECONDARY COVERAGE: Zero coverage. The free safety and Whip cover the running backs, and the strong safety covers the tight end.

STUD: Rushes from the edge. Contains the quarterback and strongside run. Chases weakside run.

BUCK: Attacks the near shoulder of the offensive tackle and secures the C gap.

STRONG SAFETY: Shuffles outside during the snap and covers the tight end.

STRONG TACKLE: Plays 3 technique.

NOSE: Plays 0 technique.

WEAK TACKLE: Plays 3 technique.

WEAK END: Plays 7 technique versus run. Contains the quarterback versus pass.

WHIP: Plays base technique versus run. Covers the near back versus pass.

FREE SAFETY: Creeps toward the line during cadence and threatens a strongside blitz. Pursues both strongside and weakside run from an inside-out position and covers the strongside halfback versus pass.

STRONG CORNER: Covers the flanker (inside technique).

WEAK CORNER: Covers the split end (inside technique).

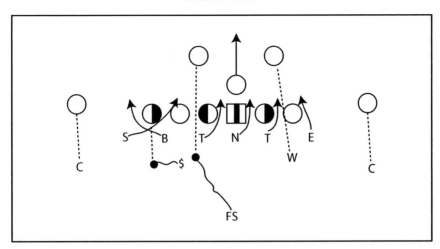

STUNT DESCRIPTION: This blitz sends Buck and Stud, features a *fake secondary blitz*, and provides the defense with a weakside line slant.

SECONDARY COVERAGE: Zero coverage. The free safety and Whip cover the running backs, and the strong safety covers the tight end.

STUD: Loops behind Buck and secures the C gap.

BUCK: Slants across the face of the tight end. Secures the D gap versus run and contains the quarterback versus pass.

STRONG SAFETY: Shuffles outside during the snap and covers the tight end.

STRONG TACKLE: Slants into the A gap.

NOSE: Slants into the weakside A gap.

WEAK TACKLE: Slants into the B gap.

WEAK END: Plays 7 technique versus run. Contains the quarterback versus pass.

WHIP: Plays base technique versus run. Covers the near back versus pass.

FREE SAFETY: Creeps toward the line during cadence and threatens a strongside blitz. Secures the B gap versus strongside run and pursues weakside run from an inside-out position. Covers the strongside halfback versus pass.

STRONG CORNER: Covers the flanker (inside technique).

WEAK CORNER: Covers the split end (inside technique).

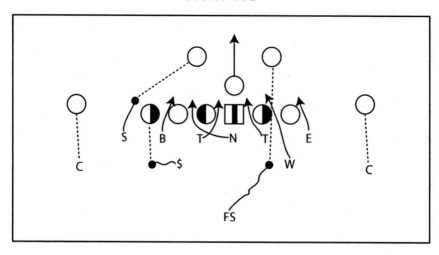

STUNT DESCRIPTION: This blitz sends Buck and Whip, features a *fake secondary blitz*, and provides the defense with a strongside line twist.

SECONDARY COVERAGE: Zero coverage. The free safety and Stud cover the running backs, and the strong safety covers the tight end.

STUD: Convinces the offense that he's rushing from the edge. Contains strongside run, chases weakside run, and spies the near back versus pass.

BUCK: Attacks the near shoulder of the offensive tackle. Secures the C gap versus run and contains the quarterback versus pass.

STRONG SAFETY: Shuffles outside during the snap and covers the tight end.

STRONG TACKLE: Slants into the A gap.

NOSE: Loops behind the strong tackle into the strongside B gap.

WEAK TACKLE: Slants into the A gap.

WEAK END: Plays 7 technique versus run. Contains the quarterback versus pass.

WHIP: Blitzes through the B gap.

FREE SAFETY: Creeps toward the line during cadence and threatens a weakside blitz. Scrapes outside and contains versus weakside run. Pursues weakside run from an inside-out position and covers the weakside halfback versus pass.

STRONG CORNER: Covers the flanker (inside technique).

WEAK CORNER: Covers the split end (inside technique).

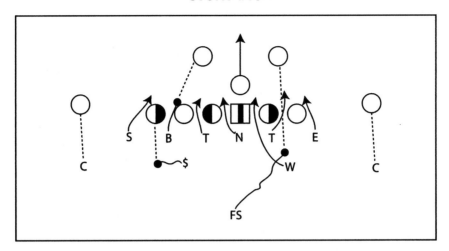

STUNT DESCRIPTION: This blitz sends Stud and Whip while featuring a *fake secondary blitz*.

SECONDARY COVERAGE: Zero coverage. The free safety and Buck cover the running backs, and the strong safety covers the tight end.

STUD: Rushes from the edge. Contains the quarterback and strongside run. Chases weakside run.

BUCK: Attacks the near shoulder of the offensive tackle. Secures the C gap versus run and spies the near back versus pass.

STRONG SAFETY: Shuffles outside during the snap and covers the tight end.

STRONG TACKLE: Slants to the B gap.

NOSE: Slants to the strongside A gap.

WEAK TACKLE: Slants to the B gap.

WEAK END: Plays 7 technique versus run. Contains the quarterback versus pass.

WHIP: Blitzes through the weakside A gap.

FREE SAFETY: Creeps toward the line during cadence and threatens a weakside blitz. Scrapes outside and contains versus weakside run. Pursues weakside run from an inside-out position and covers the weakside halfback versus pass.

STRONG CORNER: Covers the flanker (inside technique).

WEAK CORNER: Covers the split end (inside technique).

STUNT #80

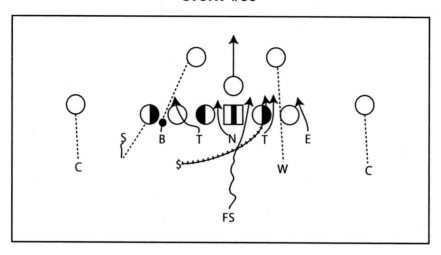

STUNT DESCRIPTION: This weakside overload features a *secondary blitz.*

SECONDARY COVERAGE: Zero coverage. Whip and Buck cover the running backs, and Stud covers the tight end.

STUD: Creeps back during cadence and covers the tight end.

BUCK: Plays 7 technique versus run and spies the near back versus pass.

STRONG SAFETY: Plays base technique versus run. Delay blitzes (twin stunt) through the weakside B gap versus pass.

STRONG TACKLE: Slants to the B gap. Secures this gap versus run and contain rushes versus pass.

NOSE: Slants to the strongside A gap.

WEAK TACKLE: Slants to the B gap.

WEAK END: Plays 7 technique versus run. Contains the quarterback versus pass.

WHIP: Plays base technique versus run. Covers the near back versus pass.

FREE SAFETY: Creeps toward the line during cadence and blitzes through the weakside A gap at the snap.

STRONG CORNER: Covers the flanker (inside technique).

WEAK CORNER: Covers the split end (inside technique).

STUNT #81

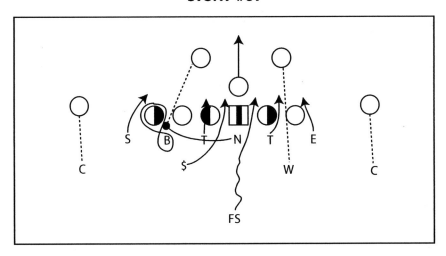

STUNT DESCRIPTION: This *secondary blitz* gives the *illusion* that the defense is *sending the house*.

SECONDARY COVERAGE: Zero coverage. Whip and nose cover the running backs, and Buck covers the tight end.

STUD: Rushes from the edge. Contains the quarterback and strongside run. Chases weakside run.

BUCK: Covers the tight end.

STRONG SAFETY: Blitzes through the strongside A gap.

STRONG TACKLE: Plays 3 technique.

NOSE: Slants to the far shoulder of the offensive tackle. Secures the strongside C gap versus run and spies the near back versus pass.

WEAK TACKLE: Plays 3 technique.

WEAK END: Plays 7 technique versus run. Contains the quarterback versus pass.

WHIP: Plays base technique versus run. Covers the near back versus pass.

FREE SAFETY: Creeps toward the line during cadence and blitzes through the weakside A gap at the snap.

STRONG CORNER: Covers the flanker (inside technique).

WEAK CORNER: Covers the split end (inside technique).

STUNT #82

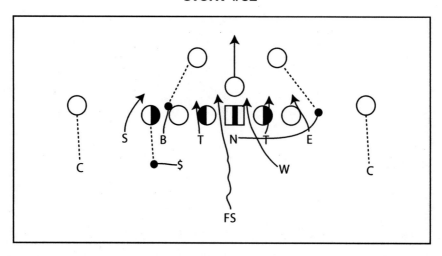

STUNT DESCRIPTION: This *secondary blitz* sends the free safety, Stud, and Whip and gives the *illusion* that the defense is *sending the house.*

SECONDARY COVERAGE: Zero coverage. Buck and nose cover the running backs, and the strong safety covers the tight end.

STUD: Rushes from the edge. Contains the quarterback and strongside run. Chases weakside run.

BUCK: Attacks the near shoulder of the offensive tackle. Secures the C gap versus run and spies the near back versus pass.

STRONG SAFETY: Shuffles outside during the snap and covers the tight end.

STRONG TACKLE: Plays 3 technique.

NOSE: Slants to the weakside D gap. Secures this gap versus run and spies the near back versus pass.

WEAK TACKLE: Plays 3 technique.

WEAK END: Attacks the near shoulder of the offensive tackle. Controls the C gap versus run and contains the quarterback versus pass.

WHIP: Blitzes through the weakside A gap.

FREE SAFETY: Creeps toward the line during cadence and blitzes through the strongside A gap at the snap.

STRONG CORNER: Covers the flanker (inside technique).

WEAK CORNER: Covers the split end (inside technique).

STUNT #83

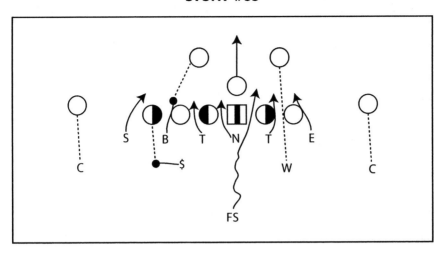

STUNT DESCRIPTION: This *secondary blitz* sends the free safety and Stud.

SECONDARY COVERAGE: Zero coverage. Buck and Whip cover the running backs, and the strong safety covers the tight end.

STUD: Rushes from the edge. Contains the quarterback and strongside run. Chases weakside run.

BUCK: Attacks the near shoulder of the offensive tackle. Secures the C gap versus run and spies the near back versus pass.

STRONG SAFETY: Shuffles outside during the snap and covers the tight end.

STRONG TACKLE: Slants into the B gap.

NOSE: Slants to the strongside A gap

WEAK TACKLE: Plays 3 technique.

WEAK END: Plays 7 technique versus run. Contains the quarterback versus pass.

WHIP: Plays base technique versus run. Covers the near back versus pass.

FREE SAFETY: Creeps toward the line during cadence and blitzes through the weakside A gap at the snap.

STRONG CORNER: Covers the flanker (inside technique).

WEAK CORNER: Covers the split end (inside technique).

STUNT #84

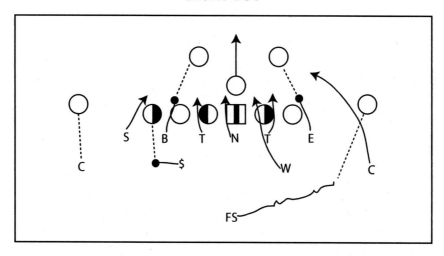

STUNT DESCRIPTION: This weakside *cornerback blitz* gives the offense the *illusion* of a 4-man weakside rush. It can only be used when the split end is aligned into the boundary or has assumed a tight split.

SECONDARY COVERAGE: Zero coverage. Buck and the weak end cover the running backs, and the strong safety covers the tight end.

STUD: Rushes from the edge. Contains the quarterback and strongside run. Chases weakside run.

BUCK: Attacks the near shoulder of the offensive tackle. Secures the C gap versus run and spies the near back versus pass.

STRONG SAFETY: Shuffles outside during the snap and covers the tight end.

STRONG TACKLE: Slants into the B gap.

NOSE: Slants to the strongside A gap

WEAK TACKLE: Slants into the B gap.

WEAK END: Attacks the near shoulder of the offensive tackle. Secures the C gap versus run and spies the near back versus pass.

WHIP: Blitzes through the weakside A gap.

FREE SAFETY: Creeps to a position that enables him to cover the split end at the snap.

STRONG CORNER: Covers the flanker (inside technique).

WEAK CORNER: Creeps inside during cadence and blitzes from the edge. Contains the quarterback and weakside run. Chases strongside run.

STUNT #85

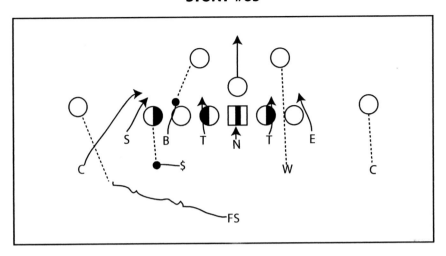

STUNT DESCRIPTION: This strongside *cornerback blitz* can only be used when Z is aligned into the boundary or has assumed a tight split.

SECONDARY COVERAGE: Zero coverage. Buck and Whip cover the running backs, and the strong safety covers the tight end.

STUD: Rushes from the edge. Contains the quarterback and strongside run. Chases weakside run.

BUCK: Attacks the near shoulder of the offensive tackle. Secures the C gap versus run and spies the near back versus pass.

STRONG SAFETY: Shuffles outside during the snap and covers the tight end.

STRONG TACKLE: Plays 3 technique.

NOSE: Plays 0 technique.

WEAK TACKLE: Plays 3 technique.

WEAK END: Plays 7 technique versus run. Contains the quarterback versus pass.

WHIP: Plays base technique versus run. Covers the near back versus pass.

FREE SAFETY: Lines up as though he's playing cover 1 and then creeps to a position that enables him to cover the flanker at the snap.

STRONG CORNER: Creeps inside during cadence and blitzes from the edge. Contains the quarterback and strongside run. Chases weakside run.

WEAK CORNER: Covers the split end (inside technique).

CHAPTER 7

Adapting Stunt Tactics to Ace and Empty Formations

STUNT #86

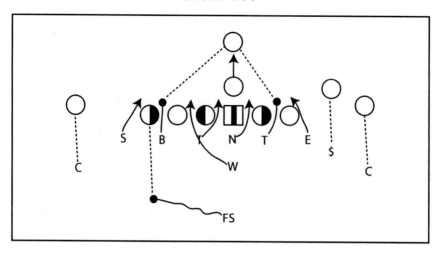

STUNT DESCRIPTION: This blitz gives the offense the *illusion* of a 7-man pass rush.

SECONDARY COVERAGE: Zero coverage disguised as cover 1. Buck and the weak tackle spy Ace.

STUD: Rushes from the edge. Contains the quarterback and strongside run. Chases weakside run.

BUCK: Plays 7 technique versus run. Spies the near back versus pass. *Note:* Buck only spies Ace if he blocks strong. If Ace blocks weak, the weak tackle covers him and Buck rushes the quarterback.

STRONG SAFETY: Strong safety is the *adjuster*. Covers receiver #2 weak (inside technique).

STRONG TACKLE: Slants to the A gap.

NOSE: Slants to the weakside A gap.

WEAK TACKLE: Slants to the B gap. Secures this gap versus run and spies Ace versus pass. *Note:* Weak tackle only spies Ace if he blocks weak. If Ace blocks strong, Buck will cover him and the weak tackle rushes the quarterback.

WEAK END: Plays 7 technique versus run. Contains the quarterback versus pass.

WHIP: Lines up as a middle linebacker and blitzes the strongside B gap.

FREE SAFETY: Covers the tight end. Disguises his assignment as cover 1.

STRONG CORNER: Covers the flanker (inside technique).

WEAK CORNER: Covers the split end (inside technique).

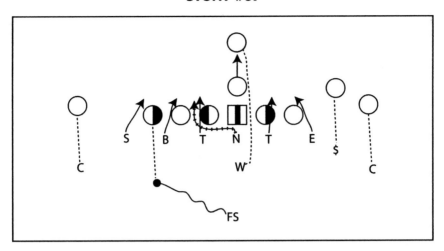

STUNT DESCRIPTION: This blitz provides the defense with a delayed twin stunt that creates a strongside overload versus pass.

SECONDARY COVERAGE: Zero coverage disguised as cover 1. Whip covers Ace.

STUD: Rushes from the edge. Contains the quarterback and strongside run. Chases weakside run.

BUCK: Attacks the near shoulder of the offensive tackle and controls the C gap.

STRONG SAFETY: The strong safety is the *adjuster*. Covers receiver #2 weak (inside technique).

STRONG TACKLE: Plays 3 technique.

NOSE: Plays 0 technique versus run. Loops into the strongside B gap (twin stunt) versus pass.

WEAK TACKLE: Plays 3 technique.

WEAK END: Plays 7 technique versus run. Contains the quarterback versus pass.

WHIP: Lines up as a middle linebacker. Pursues both strongside and weakside run from an inside-out position. Covers Ace versus pass.

FREE SAFETY: Covers the tight end. Disguises his assignment as cover 1.

STRONG CORNER: Covers the flanker (inside technique).

WEAK CORNER: Covers the split end (inside technique).

STUNT #88

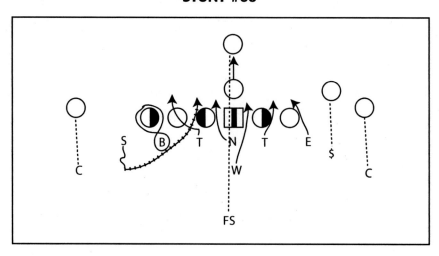

STUNT DESCRIPTION: This blitz provides the defense with a delayed linebacker blitz versus pass. It is a good run-situation stunt.

SECONDARY COVERAGE: A variation of zero coverage disguised as cover 1. The free safety covers Ace and Buck covers the tight end.

STUD: Sinks back during cadence and gives the impression that he's covering the tight end. Plays 8 technique versus run. Delay blitzes through the strongside B gap versus pass.

BUCK: Covers the tight end.

STRONG SAFETY: The strong safety is the *adjuster*. Covers receiver #2 weak (inside technique).

STRONG TACKLE: Slants to the B gap and secures this gap versus run. Contain rushes versus pass.

NOSE: Slants to the strongside A gap.

WEAK TACKLE: Slants to the B gap.

WEAK END: Plays 7 technique versus run. Contains the quarterback versus pass.

WHIP: Lines up as a middle linebacker. Blitzes through the weakside A gap at the snap.

FREE SAFETY: Covers Ace. Disguises his assignment as cover 1 *or* pretends to be on a safety blitz by creeping toward the line during cadence.

STRONG CORNER: Covers the flanker (inside technique).

WEAK CORNER: Covers the split end (inside technique).

STUNT #89

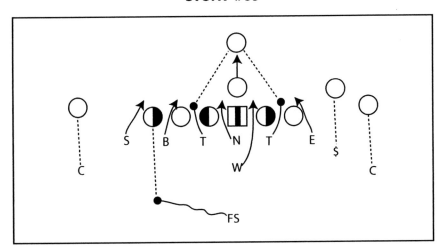

STUNT DESCRIPTION: This blitz provides the defense with the *illusion* of a 7-man pass rush.

SECONDARY COVERAGE: Zero coverage disguised as cover 1. The free safety covers the tight end and both tackles spy Ace.

STUD: Rushes from the edge. Contains the quarterback and strongside run. Chases weakside run.

BUCK: Attacks the near shoulder of the offensive tackle and controls the C gap.

STRONG SAFETY: The strong safety is the *adjuster*. Covers receiver #2 weak (inside technique).

STRONG TACKLE: Slants to the B gap. Secures this gap versus run and spies Ace versus pass. *Note:* The strong tackle only spies Ace if he blocks strong. If Ace blocks weak, the weak tackle covers him and the strong tackle rushes the quarterback.

NOSE: Slants to the strongside A gap.

WEAK TACKLE: Slants to the B gap. Secures this gap versus run and spies Ace versus pass. *Note:* The weak tackle only spies Ace if he blocks weak. If Ace blocks strong, the strong tackle covers him and the weak tackle rushes the quarterback.

WEAK END: Plays 7 technique versus run. Contains the quarterback versus pass.

WHIP: Lines up as a middle linebacker. Blitzes through the weakside A gap at the snap.

FREE SAFETY: Covers the tight end. Disguises his assignment as cover 1.

STRONG CORNER: Covers the flanker (inside technique).

WEAK CORNER: Covers the split end (inside technique).

STUNT #90

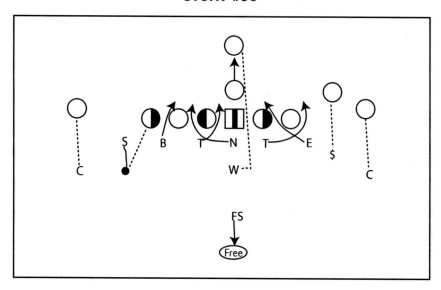

STUNT DESCRIPTION: This dog sends Buck and is enhanced by a double line twist.

SECONDARY COVERAGE: Cover 1. Stud covers the tight end, Whip covers Ace, and the free safety plays center field.

STUD: Sinks back during cadence. Plays 8 technique versus run. Covers the tight end versus pass.

BUCK: Attacks the near shoulder of the offensive tackle. Secures the C gap versus run and contains the quarterback versus pass.

STRONG SAFETY: The strong safety is the *adjuster*. Covers receiver #2 weak (inside technique).

STRONG TACKLE: Slants into the A gap.

NOSE: Loops behind the strong tackle into the strongside B gap.

WEAK TACKLE: Loops behind the weak end and attacks the outside shoulder of the offensive tackle. Secures the C gap versus run and contains the quarterback versus pass.

WEAK END: Slants into the B gap.

WHIP: Lines up as a middle linebacker. Pursues both strongside and weakside run from an inside-out position. Covers Ace versus pass.

FREE SAFETY: Lines up as though he's playing cover 3. Provides alley support versus run. Plays center field versus pass.

STRONG CORNER: Covers receiver #1 (inside/outside technique dependent upon field position and the distance of the flanker's split).

WEAK CORNER: Covers receiver #1 (inside/outside technique dependent upon field position and the distance of the split end's split).

STUNT #91

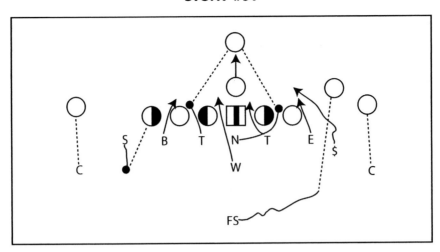

STUNT DESCRIPTION: This blitz provides the defense with a strong safety blitz and gives the offense the *illusion* of a 4-man weakside pass rush.

SECONDARY COVERAGE: A variation of zero coverage. Stud covers the tight end and the strong tackle and nose spy Ace.

STUD: Sinks back during cadence and covers the tight end.

BUCK: Attacks the near shoulder of the offensive tackle. Controls the C gap versus run and contains the quarterback versus pass.

STRONG SAFETY: Adjusts to receiver #2 weak. Creeps inside during cadence and blitzes from the edge. Contains the quarterback and weakside run. Chases strongside run.

STRONG TACKLE: Slants to the B gap. Secures this gap versus run and spies Ace versus pass. *Note:* The strong tackle only spies Ace if he blocks strong. If Ace blocks weak, the nose covers him and the strong tackle rushes the quarterback.

NOSE: Loops behind the weal tackle to the weakside B gap. Secures this gap versus run and spies Ace versus pass. *Note:* Nose only spies Ace if he blocks weak. If Ace blocks strong, the strong tackle covers him and the nose rushes the quarterback.

WEAK TACKLE: Slants into the A gap.

WEAK END: Plays 7 technique.

WHIP: Lines up as a middle linebacker and blitzes through the strongside a gap.

FREE SAFETY: Lines up as though he's playing cover 1, but creeps to a position that enables him to cover receiver #2 weak at the snap (inside technique).

STRONG CORNER: Covers the flanker (inside technique).

WEAK CORNER: Covers the split end (inside technique).

STUNT #92

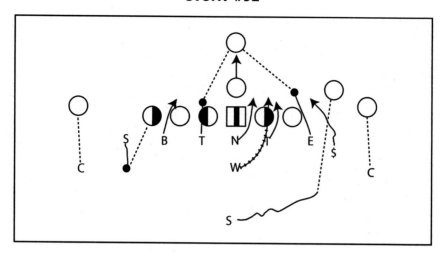

STUNT DESCRIPTION: This *strong safety blitz* is enhanced by a delayed blitz by Whip (twin stunt), which creates a weakside overload.

SECONDARY COVERAGE: A variation of zero coverage. Stud covers the tight end and the strong tackle and weak end spy Ace.

STUD: Sinks back during cadence and covers the tight end.

BUCK: Attacks the near shoulder of the offensive tackle. Controls the C gap versus run and contains the quarterback versus pass.

STRONG SAFETY: Adjusts to receiver #2 weak. Creeps inside during cadence and blitzes from the edge at the snap. Contains the quarterback and weakside run. Chases strongside run.

STRONG TACKLE: Plays 3 technique versus run and spies Ace versus pass. *Note:* The strong tackle only spies Ace if he blocks strong. If Ace blocks weak, the weak end covers him and the strong tackle rushes the quarterback.

NOSE: Slants into the weakside A gap.

WEAK TACKLE: Slants into the B gap.

WEAK END: Plays 7 technique versus run. Spies the near back versus pass. *Note:* The weak end only spies Ace if he blocks weak. If Ace blocks strong, the strong tackle covers him and the weak end rushes the quarterback.

WHIP: Lines up as a middle linebacker. Pursues run from an inside-out position. Delay blitzes through the weakside A gap (twin stunt) versus pass.

FREE SAFETY: Lines up as though he's playing cover 1, but creeps to a position that enables him to cover receiver #2 weak at the snap (inside technique).

STRONG CORNER: Covers the flanker (inside technique).

WEAK CORNER: Covers the split end (inside technique).

STUNT #93

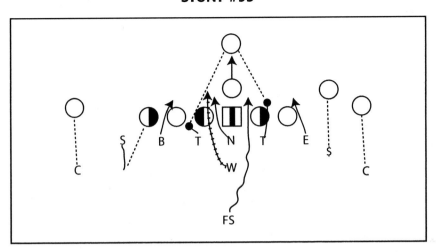

STUNT DESCRIPTION: This blitz provides the defense with a free safety blitz and a delayed linebacker blitz.

SECONDARY COVERAGE: A variation of zero coverage. Stud covers the tight end and both tackles spy Ace.

STUD: Sinks back during cadence and covers the tight end.

BUCK: Attacks the near shoulder of the offensive tackle. Controls the C gap versus run and contains the quarterback versus pass.

STRONG SAFETY: The strong safety is the *adjuster*. Covers receiver #2 weak (inside technique).

STRONG TACKLE: Slants to the B gap. Secures this gap versus run and spies Ace versus pass. *Note:* The strong tackle only spies Ace if he blocks strong. If Ace blocks weak, the weak tackle covers him and the strong tackle rushes the quarterback.

NOSE: Slants into the strongside A gap.

WEAK TACKLE: Slants to the B gap. Secures this gap versus run and spies Ace versus pass. *Note:* The weak tackle only spies Ace if he blocks weak. If Ace blocks strong, the strong tackle covers him and the weak tackle rushes the quarterback.

WEAK END: Plays 7 technique versus run. Contains the quarterback versus pass.

WHIP: Lines up as a middle linebacker and pursues both strongside and weakside run from an inside-out position. Blitzes through the face of the strongside offensive guard versus pass.

FREE SAFETY: Lines up as though he's playing cover 1 but creeps toward the line during cadence and blitzes through the weakside A gap at the snap.

STRONG CORNER: Covers the flanker (inside technique).

WEAK CORNER: Covers the split end (inside technique).

STUNT #94

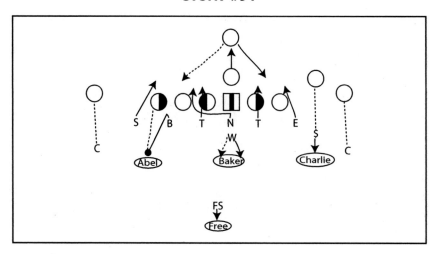

STUNT DESCRIPTION: This *fire zone blitz* sends Stud, and provides the defense with a strongside twin stunt.

SECONDARY COVERAGE: Cover 1. Buck, Whip and the strong safety drop into coverage and the free safety plays center field.

STUD: Rushes from the edge. Contains the quarterback and strongside run. Chases weakside run.

BUCK: Plays 7 technique versus run. Drops **Abel** versus pass. *Note:* Buck must key Ace during his drop. If Ace blocks strong, Buck works an **Abel-Baker** combo with Whip, but if Ace blocks weak, Buck must cover the tight end by himself.

STRONG SAFETY: Adjusts to receiver #2 weak. Keys Ace as the ball is being snapped. If Ace blocks weak, the strong safety works a **Charlie-Baker** combo with Whip, but if Ace blocks strong, the strong safety must cover receiver #2 by himself.

STRONG TACKLE: Plays 3 technique.

NOSE: Plays 0 technique versus run. Loops into the strongside B gap (twin stunt) versus pass.

WEAK TACKLE: Plays 3 technique.

WEAK END: Plays 7 technique versus run. Contains the quarterback versus pass.

WHIP: Lines up as a middle linebacker. Pursues both strongside and weakside run from an inside-out position. Drops **Baker** versus pass. *Note:* The direction of Ace's block determines the direction of Whip's drop. If Ace blocks strong, Whip works an **Abel-Baker** combo with Buck, but if Ace blocks weak, Whip works a **Baker-Charlie** combo with the strong safety.

FREE SAFETY: Lines up as though he's playing cover 3. Provides alley support versus run. Plays center field versus pass.

STRONG CORNER: Covers #1 (inside/outside technique dependent upon field position and the distance of the flanker's split).

WEAK CORNER: Covers #1 (inside/outside technique dependent upon field position and the distance of the split end's split).

STUNT #95

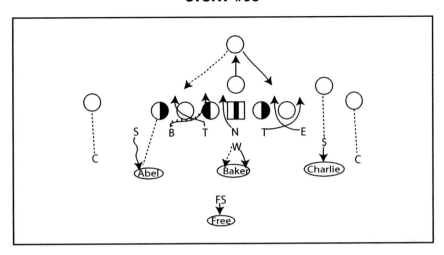

STUNT DESCRIPTION: This *fire zone blitz* sends Buck on a delayed blitz versus pass and is enhanced by a double line twist.

SECONDARY COVERAGE: Cover 1. Stud, Whip and the strong safety drop into coverage and the free safety plays center field.

STUD: Plays 8 technique versus run. Drops **Abel** versus pass. *Note:* Stud must key Ace during his drop. If Ace blocks strong, Stud works an **Abel-Baker** combo with Whip, but if Ace blocks weak, Stud must cover the tight end by himself.

BUCK: Plays 7 technique versus run. Loops behind the strong tackle into the B gap versus pass.

STRONG SAFETY: Adjusts to receiver #2 weak. Keys Ace as the ball is being snapped. If Ace blocks weak, the strong safety works a **Charlie-Baker** combo with Whip, but if Ace blocks strong, the strong safety must cover receiver #2 by himself.

STRONG TACKLE: Plays 3 technique versus run. Contain rushes versus pass.

NOSE: Slants into the strongside A gap.

WEAK TACKLE: Loops behind the weak end and attacks the outside shoulder of the offensive tackle. Secures the C gap versus run and contains the quarterback versus pass.

WEAK END: Slants into the B gap.

WHIP: Lines up as a middle linebacker. Pursues both strongside and weakside run from an inside-out position. Drops **Baker** versus pass. *Note:* The direction of Ace's block determines the direction of Whip's drop. If Ace blocks strong, Whip works an **Abel-Baker** combo with Stud, but if Ace blocks weak, Whip works a **Baker-Charlie** combo with the strong safety.

FREE SAFETY: Lines up as though he's playing cover 3. Provides alley support versus run. Plays center field versus pass.

STRONG CORNER: Covers #1 (inside/outside technique dependent upon field position and the distance of the flanker's split).

WEAK CORNER: Covers #1 (inside/outside technique dependent upon field position and the distance of the split end's split).

STUNT #96

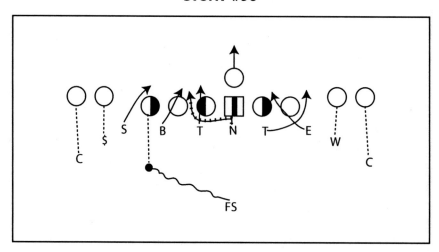

STUNT DESCRIPTION: This blitz provides the defense with a delayed twin stunt that creates a strongside overload versus an empty set.

SECONDARY COVERAGE: Zero coverage disguised as cover 1.

STUD: Rushes from the edge. Contains the quarterback and strongside run. Chases weakside run.

BUCK: Attacks the near shoulder of the offensive tackle and controls the C gap.

STRONG SAFETY: Covers receiver #2 strong (inside technique).

STRONG TACKLE: Plays 3 technique.

NOSE: Plays 0 technique versus run. Loops into the strongside B gap (twin stunt) versus pass.

WEAK TACKLE: Loops behind the weak end and attacks the outside shoulder of the offensive tackle. Secures the C gap versus run and contains the quarterback versus pass.

WEAK END: Slants into the B gap.

WHIP: Covers receiver #2 weak (inside technique).

FREE SAFETY: Covers the tight end. Disguises his assignment as cover 1.

STRONG CORNER: Covers the flanker (inside technique).

WEAK CORNER: Covers the split end (inside technique).

STUNT #97

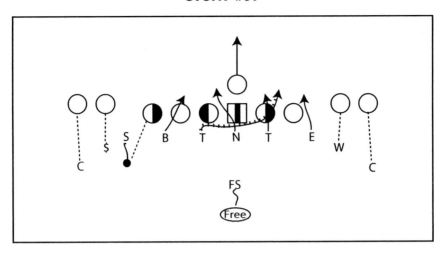

STUNT DESCRIPTION: This *dog* sends Buck and provides the defense with a delayed twin stunt that creates a weakside overload.

SECONDARY COVERAGE: Cover 1.

STUD: Sinks back during cadence. Plays 8 technique versus run. Covers the tight end versus pass.

BUCK: Attacks the near shoulder of the offensive tackle. Secures the C gap versus run and contains the quarterback versus pass.

STRONG SAFETY: Covers receiver #2 strong (inside technique).

STRONG TACKLE: Plays 3 technique versus run. Loops into the weak side B gap versus pass.

NOSE: Plays 0 technique versus run. Slowly works his way through the strongside A gap versus pass.

WEAK TACKLE: Plays 3 technique.

WEAK END: Plays 7 technique versus run. Contains the quarterback versus pass.

WHIP: Covers receiver #2 weak (inside technique).

FREE SAFETY: Lines up as though he's playing cover 3. Provides alley support versus run. Plays center field versus pass.

STRONG CORNER: Covers receiver #1 (inside/outside technique dependent upon field position and the distance of the flanker's split).

WEAK CORNER: Covers receiver #1 (inside/outside technique dependent upon field position and the distance of the split end's split).

STUNT #98

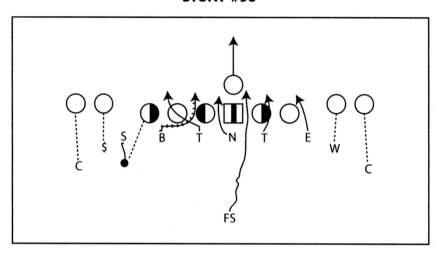

STUNT DESCRIPTION: This blitz provides the defense with a *free safety blitz* and a delayed strongside linebacker/line twist.

SECONDARY COVERAGE: A variation of zero coverage. Stud covers the tight end.

STUD: Sinks back during cadence and covers the tight end.

BUCK: Plays 7 technique versus run. Loops behind the strong tackle and rushes through the strongside B gap versus pass.

STRONG SAFETY: Covers receiver #2 strong (inside technique).

STRONG TACKLE: Plays 3 technique versus run. Contain rushes versus pass.

NOSE: Slants into the strongside A gap.

WEAK TACKLE: Plays 3 technique.

WEAK END: Plays 7 technique versus run. Contains the quarterback versus pass.

WHIP: Covers receiver #2 weak (inside technique).

FREE SAFETY: Lines up as though he's playing cover 1 but creeps toward the line during cadence and blitzes through the weakside A gap at the snap.

STRONG CORNER: Covers the flanker (inside technique).

WEAK CORNER: Covers the split end (inside technique).

STUNT #99

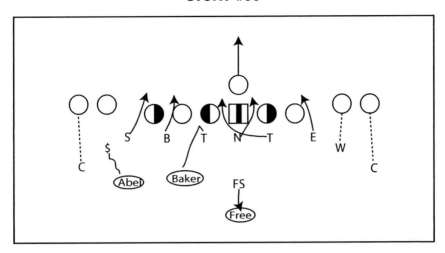

STUNT DESCRIPTION: This is a variation of the *fire zone blitz* sends both Buck and Stud and provides the defense with a strongside line twist.

SECONDARY COVERAGE: Cover 1. The strong tackle and the strong safety drop into coverage and combo-cover receiver #2 strong and the tight end. The free safety plays center field.

STUD: Rushes from the edge. Contains the quarterback and strongside run. Chases weakside run.

BUCK: Attacks the near shoulder of the offensive tackle and controls the C gap.

STRONG SAFETY: Adjusts to #2 strong. Drops **Abel** and combo-covers receiver #2 strong and the tight end with the strongside tackle versus pass.

STRONG TACKLE: Plays 3 technique versus run. Drops **Baker** and combo-covers receiver #2 strong and the tight end with the strong safety versus pass.

NOSE: Slants into the weakside A gap.

WEAK TACKLE: Loops behind the nose into the strongside A gap.

WEAK END: Plays 7 technique versus run. Contains the quarterback versus pass.

WHIP: Covers receiver #2 weak (inside technique).

FREE SAFETY: Lines up as though he's playing cover 3. Provides alley support versus run. Plays center field versus pass.

STRONG CORNER: Covers receiver #1 (inside/outside technique dependent upon field position and the distance of the flanker's split).

WEAK CORNER: Covers receiver #1 (inside/outside technique dependent upon field position and the distance of the split end's split).

STUNT #100

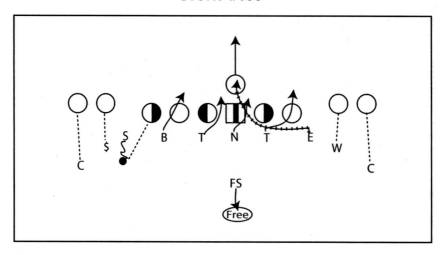

STUNT DESCRIPTION: This *dog* sends Buck and provides the defense with a weakside delayed twin stunt versus pass.

SECONDARY COVERAGE: Cover 1.

STUD: Sinks back during cadence. Plays 8 technique versus run. Covers the tight end versus pass.

BUCK: Attacks the near shoulder of the offensive tackle. Secures the C gap versus run and contains the quarterback versus pass.

STRONG SAFETY: Covers receiver #2 strong (inside technique).

STRONG TACKLE: Slants into the A gap.

NOSE: Slants into the weakside A gap.

WEAK TACKLE: Plays 3 technique versus run. Contain rushes versus pass.

WEAK END: Plays 7 technique versus run. Loops behind the weak tackle into the weakside A gap (twin stunt) versus pass.

WHIP: Covers receiver #2 weak (inside technique).

FREE SAFETY: Lines up as though he's playing cover 3. Provides alley support versus run. Plays center field versus pass.

STRONG CORNER: Covers receiver #1 (inside/outside technique dependent upon field position and the distance of the flanker's split).

WEAK CORNER: Covers receiver #1 (inside/outside technique dependent upon field position and the distance of the split end's split).

STUNT #101

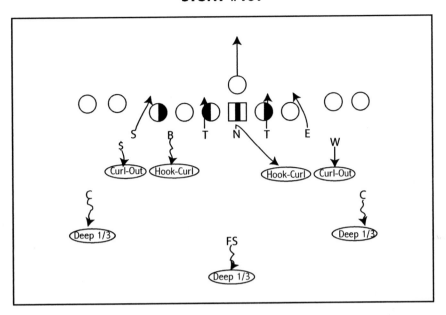

STUNT DESCRIPTION: This is an *old school zone blitz*.

SECONDARY COVERAGE: Cover 3.

STUD: Rushes from the edge. Contains the quarterback and strongside run. Chases weakside run.

BUCK: Plays 7 technique versus run. Drops hook-curl versus pass.

STRONG SAFETY: Adjusts to receiver #2 strong and drops curl-out versus pass.

STRONG TACKLE: Plays 3 technique.

NOSE: Plays 0 technique versus run. Drops hook-curl versus pass.

WEAK TACKLE: Plays 3 technique.

WEAK END: Plays 7 technique versus run. Contains the quarterback versus pass.

WHIP: Adjusts to receiver #2 weak and drops curl-out versus pass.

FREE SAFETY: Covers the deep middle third.

STRONG CORNER: Covers the deep outside third.

WEAK CORNER: Covers the deep outside third.

CHAPTER 8

A Synopsis of Bear 46 Base Responsibilities

Strong/Weak Tackle

Stance & Alignment

Player takes a 3- or 4-point stance, inside foot back, and plays 3 technique.

Responsibilities

- *Running play toward player*: Plays B gap.
- *Running play away from player*: Squeezes the A gap.
- *Passing play*: Rushes the B gap.

Keys

- *Primary*: Guard/ball movement.
- *Secondary*: Tackle/pulling linemen.

Important Techniques/Concepts

Jet technique: Target is the guard's outside shoulder. The first step is with the inside foot. Player must maintain outside leverage and not get hooked.

Key Blocks

- *Drive block*: Player reads the guard's head, maintains outside leverage.
- *Hook block*: Player must not let the guard's head outside; he must maintain outside leverage.
- *Turn out block*: Player squeezes the A gap and looks for cutback.
- *Double team*: Player attacks the tackle. He should not get driven back.
- *Kiss block*: Player forces the double team. He prevents the tackle from blocking the linebackers.
- *Zone block*: Player plays it like a hook block. He prevents the tackle from releasing to the second level.
- *Guard blocks inside/tackle cracks*: Player jams the guard, fights pressure, and flattens across the tackle's face.
- *Guard blocks inside/tackle cut off*: Player jams the guard, keeps him of linebackers, rips through the tackle's head and pursues flat.
- *Guard blocks inside/no outside pressure*: Trap! He traps the trapper, and spills everything inside.
- *Fold*: Player penetrates the line of scrimmage if he's beaten the tackle's head; otherwise, he flattens across tackle's face.
- *Guard pulls outside/no outside pressure*: Trap! He traps the trapper, and spills everything inside.
- *Guard pulls inside/tackle cutoff*: Player gets into the guard's hip pocket and follows him to the point of attack.
- *Guard pulls inside/center blocks the player*: Player flattens across the center's face.

Nose

Stance & Alignment

Player takes a 3- or 4-point stance, minimum -no stagger, and plays zero technique.

Responsibilities

- *Running play toward player*: Plays play side A gap.
- *Passing play*: Rushes either A gap.

Keys

- *Primary*: Center/ball movement.
- *Secondary*: Both guards.

Important Techniques/Concepts

- Target is the center's facemask.
- *Crush technique*. Player attacks the center with hands–inside lockout. He takes short jab step in direction of play. He controls both A gaps. Player keeps his shoulders square and remembers that the pulling guards indicate point of attack.

Key Blocks

- *Drive block*: Player knocks the center back. He stays square, and tries to locate the ball.
- *Double team*: Player attacks the guard. He stays low, and must not get driven back.
- *Hook block*: Player controls the center's outside shoulder. He keeps his shoulders parallel.
- *Zone block*: Player plays it like a hook block. He keeps the center off of the linebacker.
- *Center blocks away/down block by guard*: Player releases from the center and controls the outside shoulder of the guard.
- Pass: Player rushes either A gap.

Weak End

Stance & Alignment

Player takes a 2- or 3-point stance, inside foot up, and plays a tight 7 technique (One or two yards outside of the tackle).

Responsibilities

- *Running play toward player*: Plays the C gap
- *Running play away from player*: Chases while looking for reverse, counter, and cutback.
- *Passing play*: Contains rush.

Keys

- *Primary*: Tackle/ball movement.
- *Secondary*: Near back/pulling linemen.

Important Techniques/Concepts

Jet technique: Player penetrates the line of scrimmage (one yard) at the snap. He maintains outside leverage, and must not get hooked.

Key Blocks

- *Hook block*: This block should never happen. Player must beat the tackle's head across the line of scrimmage.
- *Tackle turnout block/weakside flow*: Player uses the tackle's body to squeeze the play inside, while maintaining outside leverage.
- *Tackle turnout block/strongside flow*: Player avoids the tackle's block. He chases as deep as the ball.
- *Tackle blocks inside/no jack block*: Trap or guard/tackle cross blocks. He traps the trapper, and spills the play inside.
- *Tackle blocks inside/jack block*: Player stuffs the back into the hole. He forces the play outside.
- *Pass*: Player contains the rush.

Buck

Stance & Alignment

Player takes a 2-point stance, feet parallel, with an inside shade on the tight end (outside foot pointing at tight end's inside foot).

Responsibilities

- *Running play toward player*: Plays the C gap.
- *Running play away from player*: Depends upon coverage.
- *Passing play*: Depends upon coverage.

Keys

- *Primary*: Tight end.
- *Secondary*: Near back/pulling linemen.

Important Techniques/Concepts

Player steps with inside foot, gets his hands on the tight end and jams him. He must not get driven back or crushed inside.

Key Blocks

- *Tight end blocks player/inside play*: Player controls the tight end, plugs the C gap and forces the play inside.
- *Tight end blocks player/outside play*: Player controls the tight end, works across the tight end's face, and pursues from an inside-out position.
- *Tight end releases/tackle turnout/strongside flow*: Player uses the tackle's body to squeezes the play inside while maintaining outside leverage.
- *Tight end releases/tackle turnout/weakside flow*: Chase or cover–depends upon coverage.
- *Tight end releases/jack block*: Player squeezes the C gap attacks back on the line of scrimmage with inside forearm, and forces play inside.
- *Tight end releases/no jack block*: Trap or guard/tackle cross blocks. He squeezes the C gap, and attacks the blocker on line of scrimmage with his inside forearm, and spills the play inside.
- *Tight end releases/pass*: Player contain rushes or covers, depending upon coverage.

Stud

Stance & Alignment

Player takes a 2-point stance, inside foot up, and plays 8 technique.

Responsibilities

- *Running play toward player*: Player contains.
- *Running play away from player*: Depends upon coverage.
- *Passing play*: Depends upon coverage.

Keys

- *Primary*: Tight end/ball movement.
- *Secondary*: Near back/pulling linemen.

Important Techniques/Concepts

Depends upon coverage. If player is not involved: use Jet technique. Player penetrates the line of scrimmage (one yard) at the snap. He maintains outside leverage, and must not get hooked.

Key Blocks

- *Tight end blocks 7/near back kick out*: Off-tackle play. Player squeezes the play inside, closes tight to the tight end's block, and attacks the back with his inside forearm. He keeps his shoulders parallel to the line of scrimmage and maintains outside leverage.
- *Tight end blocks 7/near back hook block*: Sweep play. Player keeps his shoulders parallel to the line of scrimmage and maintains outside leverage. He forces the ball carrier inside or wide and deep.
- *Tight end blocks player or releases/near back blocks 7*: Off tackle play. Player squeezes the play inside, while maintaining outside leverage. Player must expect the ball carrier to break the play outside.
- *Tight end blocks player/sweep*: Player must beat the tight end's block and blow-up the play in the backfield.
- *Tight end releases/flow away*: Player chases or covers—depending upon coverage.
- *Tight end releases/pass:* Player contain rushes or covers, depending upon coverage.

Whip

Stance & Alignment

Player takes a 2-point stance, five yards deep, lined up on the inside eye of the offensive tackle. He should have a slight stagger with his outside foot back.

Responsibilities

- *Running play toward player*: Player contains.
- *Running play away from player*: Player is the Hitman. He works downhill and pursues the ball from an inside-out position.
- *Passing play*: Depends upon coverage.

Keys

- *Primary*: Backfield flow.
- *Secondary*: Weak tackle.

Important Techniques/Concepts

Player mirrors backfield flow by shuffling parallel to the line of scrimmage. He scrapes outside and contains versus weak flow. He works downhill and pursues from an inside-out position versus strong flow. He must look for cutbacks, counters, and reverses, while being prepared to plug air while in pursuit.

Attacking Blockers

Player maintains outside leverage and attacks blockers with inside forearm (using his hands versus cut block).

Strong Safety

Stance & Alignment

Player takes a 2-point stance, five yards deep, lined up on the outside shade of the offensive tackle. He maintains a slight stagger with his outside foot back.

Keys, Responsibilities, & Techniques

Same as Whip when Buck is not locked on to the tight end.

Responsibilities when Buck is locked on TE

- *Running play towards player*: Plays the C gap.

- *Running play away from player*: Player is the Hitman. He works downhill and pursues the ball from an inside-out position.

- *Passing play*: Depends upon coverage.

Keys when Buck is locked on TE

- *Primary*: Tackle.

- *Secondary*: Backfield flow.

Important Techniques/Concepts

Player attacks blockers with inside forearm, while maintaining outside leverage and keeping his shoulders parallel to the line of scrimmage.

Key Blocks

- *Tackle base block*: Player attacks the tackle with an inside forearm and shoulder, while maintaining outside leverage.

- *Tackle down block*: Player steps up quickly and takes on the lead back or pulling lineman with his inside shoulder and forearm.

- *Tackle out block*: Player steps up quickly and takes on the lead back or pulling lineman with his inside shoulder and forearm.

- *Tackle cut-off block (flow away)*: Player avoids the tackle's block if possible. He works downhill and laterally (playing across the tackle's face if necessary) and pursues the play from an inside-out position.

- *Zone (flow away)/guard blocks player*: Player works downhill and across the guard's face. He pursues inside out.

- *Tackle pulls inside*: Player works downhill and pursues inside out.

- *Tackle pulls outside:* Player scrapes outside, and pursues the ball from an inside-out position.

- *Tackle pass blocks*: Depends upon coverage.

ABOUT THE AUTHORS

Leo Hand is the defensive coordinator at El Paso (TX) High School, a position he assumed in 2001. Prior to that, he held the same job at Irvin High School in El Paso, Texas. With over 33 years of experience as a teacher and coach, Hand has served in a variety of coaching positions in his career. At each stop, he has achieved a notable level of success.

A graduate of Emporia State University in Emporia, Kansas, Hand began his football coaching career in 1968 as the junior varsity coach at McQuaid Jesuit High School in Rochester, New York. After two seasons, he then accepted the job as the offensive line coach at Aquinas Institute (1970-'71). Next, he served as the head coach at Saint John Fisher College—a position he held for two years. He has also served on the gridiron staffs at APW (Parrish, NY) High School (head coach); Saint Anthony (Long Beach, CA) High School (head coach), Daniel Murphy (Los Angeles, CA) High School (head coach), Servite (Anaheim, CA) High School (head coach); Serra (Gardena, CA) High School (head coach); Long Beach (CA) City College (offensive line and linebackers); and Los Angeles (CA) Harbor College (offensive coordinator).

During the last six years that he spent coaching interscholastic teams in California, Hand's squads won 81 percent of their games in the highly competitive area of Southern California. At Serra High School, his teams compiled a 24-1 record, won a CIF championship, and were declared California State champions. On numerous occasions, he has helped rebuild several floundering gridiron teams into highly successful programs. For his efforts, he has been honored on numerous occasions with Coach-of-the-Year recognition.

A former Golden Gloves boxing champion, Hand is a prolific author, having written several football instructional books and numerous articles that have been published. He and his wife, Mary, have nine children and seven grandchildren.

Phil Johnson, a retired attorney, was co-head coach of the Jordan High School freshman football team in Long Beach, California, during its first season (1990). Jordan competes in the highest California level of competition. Johnson also spent three seasons coaching Pop Warner football.

Johnson lives in Long Beach, CA. He has four children: sons Eric Johnson and Jeffrey Johnson, and daughters Debbie Escovedo and Carmen Waszak.